The Dream of a Broken Field

Diane Glancy

University of Nebraska Press | Lincoln and London

The Dream of a Broken Field

© 2011 by the Board of Regents
of the University of Nebraska

All rights reserved
Manufactured in the
United States of America
∞
Library of Congress
Cataloging-in-Publication Data
Glancy, Diane.
The dream of a broken field /
Diane Glancy.
    p. cm.
ISBN 978-0-8032-3481-9
(pbk. : alk. paper)
1. Glancy, Diane.
2. Authors, American—
20th century—Biography.
3. Indians of North America—
Social life and customs.
I. Title.
PS3557.L294Z465 2011
813'.54—dc22
[B]
2011013134

Designed and set in
Arno Pro by R. W. Boeche.

This book is for Joseph, Charlie, Libby, and now, Ray

Contents

Acknowledgments — xi

Book One: The Old Geography Lessons of Language
A Personal History w/Paper Dolls,
the Beginning of Travel, et al. — 1

    More Than Anything — 3
    The Names — 5
    M(other) — 6
    Black House — 8
    Outlets — 9
    The Album — 10
    Discourses on Paper Dolls — 11
    The Old Geography Lessons of Language — 17
    The Girl Made of Cotton Grass — 30
    Mukluk — 31
    Holocaust — 33
    A Book of Roads — 35

Book Two: Geographies of a Realigned Language
Native American Literature, Issues,
Ou'Wash, and Creative Theory — 45

    Flatland — 47
    Soldiers as Paper Dolls — 50
    The Paper Doll Witch Trial — 54
    Terrorists — 55

Ou'Wash	58
This Journey of Paper Dolls:	
this escape from entrapment	59
Re: The Native American Boarding School Policy	61
The Return from Carlisle	62
Boarding School Physics	65
Piecework	67
Geographies of a Realigned Language	69
The Eskimo Wars	76
Dichotomy	79

Book Three: The Dream of a Broken Field
Academia and a Sudden Retirement.
A House, a Cabin, and a Summer Trip — 83

On the Academic Front	85
I Am Wearing the Dialogue of Another	86
Costume	89
A Dress of Rain	94
A House	95
A Room	97
A Cabin	98
Intaglio	100
Rocks	105
I Pick Them Up in Travel	106
Engraved on a Rock	108
A Dock	111
The Dream of a Broken Field	113
Ascension Convention	115

Book Four: Geographies of Language
The Act and Question of Creative Nonfiction — 125

A Rocky Shelf	127
Geographies of Language	134

Buffalo Nickel	136
Sonata	137
Is not telling the truth the same as lying?	146
Penmanship: *The Return from*	
a Conference on Nonfiction	149
Off the Road	153

Book Five: One Who Wears Moths
Faith and Writing. A Continuance of Research
Trips and Travel for Teaching   157

Another Journey	159
On My Way from One Place to Another:	
On the Southern Edge of the Sandhills	
of Central Nebraska	161
Because	164
Re-entry	165
The Coldest Night in Texas	171
T(ravel)	175
The Mound Builders	178
The Shape of Privacy	185
One Who Wears Moths	187

Acknowledgments

Convergence, Autry National Center, Los Angeles, for parts of "Rocks" under the title "Stone Heart, Retrieving the Lost Voice of Sacajawea"

Hunger Mountain Journal of Art & Literature for the 2009 Nonfiction Prize to "Discourses on Paper Dolls"

Karamu for "The Old Geography Lessons of Language"

Melusine for "A Rocky Shelf"

Native Literatures: Generations, edited by John Purdy, www.nativeliteratures.com for "One Who Wears Moths"

Natural Bridge for "A Cabin"

Poets on the Psalms, edited by Lynn Domina, Trinity University Press, San Antonio, Texas, for "A Book of Roads" under the title "Upon the Floods"

Red Mountain Review for "The Return from Carlisle"

Riding Shotgun: Women Write about Their Mothers, edited by Kathryn Kysar, Borealis Books, Minnesota Historical Society Press, St. Paul, Minnesota, for "M(other)"

Riverwind for "The Mounds Builders"

Salt Magazine, Issue 2, www.saltpublishing.com/saltmagazine for "Engraved on a Rock"

[sic] A Journal of Context for "The Eskimo Wars"

Sovereign Bones, edited by Eric Gansworth, Nation Books, for "Geographies of a Realigned Language" under the title "The Bones of the Sky"

Survivance, edited by Gerald Vizenor, University of Nebraska Press, for parts of "Flatland," "The Eskimo Wars," and "Boarding School Physics" under the title "The Naked Spot: A Journey Toward Survivance"

The Tonopah Review, an Online Literary Journal for "Penmanship"

To Topos *Poetry International:* Ahani: *Indigenous American Poetry* for parts of "Flatland" under the title "Expository: Toward the Establishment of Native Theory"

Xcp Cross Cultural Poetics for "Ou'Wash" and "On My Way from One Place to Another"

Acknowledgment also to Macalester College, and Kenyon College and the Visiting Richard Thomas Professorship of Creative Writing, 2008–2009

Gratefulness to the American highways and to the state departments of transportation

The Dream of A Broken Field

Book One
The Old Geography Lessons of Language

A Personal History w/ Paper Dolls,
the Beginning of Travel, et al.

Lord, I come to you in the shadow of this waking.

More Than Anything

> Christianity, then, teaches men these two truths together: that there is a God they can know, and that there is a corruption in their nature which makes them unworthy of Him. | Pascal, *Pensées*

More than anything, I have longed for another. I remember it as a child. It has been now over six decades. I was born with a sense of abandonment I could not shake, though I lived in a house with two parents. I was on barren ground away from where I wanted to be, though I did not know where it was I wanted to be. I first heard of Jesus as a child because my parents took me to church. Probably even then I knew that Christianity would be a solace. But it was later, when marriage was difficult and I still had no where to go. I believed the gospel, though the emptiness was still with me. *I have all things. I have nothing*—That was the Apostle Paul, who expounded the gospel, a man I never really liked. What an odd religion—the relationship with someone I can't see, but believe is there. What an odd place to be a Christian—in a secular, liberal college where I can count on my hand the other Christians, as far as I know anyway. Jesus would not have received tenure there. I have no visible proof that he is, other than what happened in my life—A steady, slow pace toward faith. Jesus lived a short life, half of what I have lived. I believe in him because of a terrible need to be whole. It is because I am incomplete in myself that

I have believed. I have put weight on the words. The ear tests the word—Job 34:3. And though I felt Job's predicament from time to time, it was through the testing of words that I believe the Bible has the wholeness I sought. I had the longing for alignment to something, which turned out to be a someone. He speaks through the words of the Bible. He is the Word. I choose to believe. Though disappointment and postponement of expectation is still with me. Though I fit with no one. The Resurrection is an idea that Christ was and is again, and that one day I would return to where I wanted to be.

The Names

I am the daughter of Lewis Hall and Edith Wood Hall.
The granddaughter of William Jasper Hall and
    Orvezene Lewis Hall.
The granddaughter of Forest Kemp Wood and
    Anna Myrtle Adams Wood.

I am the great-granddaughter of Woods Lewis and
    Margaret Blevins Lewis.
Of John Hall and Matilda Hall.
Of Harvey Kemp Wood and Frances Delilah Wood.
Of James Perry Adams and Martha Adaline Adams.

Before that, it is not so clear, along the side of my
    father's family anyway.
None of these names appear in mine.

M(other)

My mother was the other in the house. She was something of which I was not part. I was left alone with her in the house until my father came home and my brother was born. A child is an island. A child is a moth. A child is a spot on the distant sea. My mother was in the house as I was. A dimmer light. An unwanted smot. I made up words for the land I inhabited. I found it moved like a floating island bumping against a continent that didn't want it bumping. I rowed my island back to the sea. Bypassing as it bypassed. What was it that was the connective? I was where I had to be when there was nowhere as yet to go. Going and ungoing. My dreams always were of travel. To speak of a mother is to speak of my father's grandfather who ran because he had to run to cover his tracks. Even his gravestone says he was born in Arkansas, but it was Indian Territory. He lied and ran, as my mother wanted the same cut and run, but I was the moth that kept her in the house. I was the cement block that tried to drown her. She swept with a broom that was her tongue. Her insistence on the mothership of which I was the dingy with cords that could be cut. I was the object to which she objected. I take this language of words though language at first is soundless. It is a longing for a connective, but it is separation that first rows across the sea. I am here. You are there. It is the first realization of (m)otherness. A filament of sound called language that could never breach the break. That took me to the shipwreck of my own motherness where my own children found the same sea. Mother of dry grass. Mother of flatlands. My mother of sharp boulders by the sea. Mother of vast loneliness and disappointment who thought she was escaping a farm, but ended up nonetheless stranded in a field. Forgive me for my attitude. I was a worse mother than she. My language was a suitcase. Forgive me, mother, for the ungraciousness of this written text. I am speaking to you as if I stood at your grave, which I have done. I know your sacrifice. I was what you didn't want to do, but did it nonetheless. You yourself were shipwrecked. Marooned. Stranded on an island you only wanted him to reach. What did you think when you married him? Idea and the actuality that surrounded that idea were different. The disappointment you received as your paycheck. Recipient of undefined sadness that was the crop on the Kansas farm where you were raised. It sent you away on a vessel. Goodbye. I look back to your formidable shore that I would never reach, but took the broken boards and made a wooden shore that almost looked like land.

Black House

It was a black hole of a house. A compressed atmosphere that pressed us flat. Our clothes hooked over our shoulders. We could not walk. But moved forward with hops, as if our feet were tied together. We were cardboard dolls in a black house, a boarding school, our mouths could not open, our lips could not part, our teeth could not show. The house was black with blue windows and a slate roof. What were our thoughts? We hopped upstairs backward. I longed for the edge of light that broke into the gray clouds that morning. Someone has done something wrong. Someone is guilty. Someone has a black heart. Someone will be punished. I am in a still room. Then I hear a rustle. Something is moving. It is a snake drawn to the heat that is my body. I am in the moment before it moves toward me, but I know it is coming. Then someone gave me something I didn't want, but said, see how you much you like it? Every failure darkened another window. Every wrongdoing put out the light in another room. One window is a black rectangle that could be a door with a step up to it. We were hobbled. We were pushed flat as tongue depressor. The tabs didn't always hold the dress. Sometimes the dress rises like a sail and flies away and I am left naked. I like it when I am riled. I like it when I have a snowy field before me and the way is not clear. I like the complexities. I swallow danger as if it were rice cakes.

Outlets

There were outlets as a child—A leaving of the house for an afternoon. There were places I went. Because at that time there were vacant lots. There were whole fields at the end of the block not yet filled with houses and stores. There were copses and sumac groves. Places I would go and sit in the small openings. What did I do all those times I went into those unfilled places? My father had made a small two-wheeled cart with a long handle. I would walk down the road pulling it behind me. My paper dolls and their clothes held down by a rock. I used leaves as plates and twigs as spoons. I served small red berries. The empty places were fields of imagination. Places where I was on my own coming away once with poison ivy so bad the doctor wasn't even sure it was poison ivy, the skin was so red and swollen with welts. Yet I returned to the twigs and leaves, the cover, the solace. It was a time away from people, a withdrawal. I didn't visit anyone with disappointment when I was there. The woods was a low covering held up by branches. A covering like a teepee of sorts. A paper doll dress.

The Album

> Those little truth serums,
> those little preachers that do not lie.
> They line up in the album like a firing squad. | Glancy, "Photography," from *The Cold-and-Hunger-Dance*

In my mother's album, there's a photograph of me standing in a neighbor's yard wearing a new dress, and holding up — on a hanger — another new one much like it. It must have been at the beginning of a new school year. Why did I choose two dresses so much alike? I was drawn to clothes. I liked the sound of the word. Clothes — Close. What you do when you go into a room and shut the door. Close it. Closet. Put it in a clause. Make a clause for it. Hide it among other meanings. Make it dependent. Later my mother said to me she wished I'd had a sister. She must have sensed my aloneness. Though I was with other clothes in the closet.

Discourses on Paper Dolls

> A paper doll is a two-dimensional figure drawn or printed on paper for which accompanying clothing has also been made. | Judy M. Johnson, *History of Paper Dolls*

I used to play with paper dolls. I don't see them in stores so much anymore. When I was a girl, there were books and books of paper dolls. Paper dolls were awkward. I had a cardboard girl, then pages of clothes to cut out with tabs on the shoulders and at the sides. The cardboard girl had a stand, so I could stand her up. It was a plastic circle with grooves or slots for her cardboard feet, or there was a cardboard fold-out piece behind her that would hold her up. Then I placed the paper clothes on her, held on with the tabs, if I didn't move her too suddenly, or play outside where the wind could carry her wardrobe away. What could I do with something so unbending, with clothes hanging on the front? What could I do without moving, or they all would tumble down?

The necessity of disguise —

You think you've got yourself covered. But your disguise is a paper dress held on by tabs over your shoulders and sides. Your whole back is open — You are cardboard. One dimensional. Don't let anyone see you from the side. Or the back. Face them head on. Know it is paper hiding you from them. You are from a broken past. You are fragments held with tabs over your shoulders. You are nothing but a visage held by a presence.

On trips I would open my book of paper dolls — take out Elaine or Patricia. I would stand them on the windowsill of the train — or the seat of the car where they would fall over. I would walk the paper dolls along a pretend street, take them to a pretend party, or pretend my way into school with them.

I would cut out new clothes for the paper dolls. I wanted the paper dolls to know transformation. I would have to work to see what was before me. I didn't take for granted without questioning. Things were never as they seemed. There was more going on than I know.

A clause is an exception.

This was the lesson at Francis Willard Elementary School where I went. There was agreement with a clause dependent on certain conditions: I could go if I was invisible. I could stay if I was quiet. I wore the childhood costumes of scarlet fever. Chicken pox. Measles. I stood in space. I was clothed in silence. I was pushed out of the house each morning.

This is more than I ever thought I could say.

Each word is a paper dress I wear on the islands of these little paragraphs.

I wear a paper dress with tabs folded over my shoulders and at my sides. I was flat as cardboard. I did not bend. I was stationary. My clothes were pieces of paper. I was a piece of paper on which to write. I walked if someone hopped me along. I was kept in a book. Tabs folded over my shoulders to hold on my clothes. No pull-ons or pullovers. I wore a disguise.

I was in a boarding school. I was not in a boarding school. I went to public school. Excuse my confusion. I was a Big Chief

Tablet. My pages were lined. I had a red line down my left margin. Why do we have margins? — Because words would slip off the page unless margins hold them on.

These pieces are my escape route.

In school, I was made to sit, though I was cardboard.

I have an uneven bend across my waist.

After school, the paper dolls could not stand up straight again.

I remember a shadow land of paper dolls — reconstructing memory that comes in fragments from time to time, or in a burst of wholeness so brief it's gone. A flash of a whole that is still only part in its almost nonexistent brief duration.

I cut out those clothes of memory for the paper dreams of the dolls.

I don't know where these words come from. These little sharpnesses that stand side by side. These *disconnectives*.

Clothing as landscape. Clothing as geography. Clothing as disguise and costume. The dialogues infested with Christianity.

I took that thread of heritage from my father, of which I knew little except it was there. I expanded it, thought about it, stood apart from it too.

I don't have the heart to battle. I think I love war more than anything.

If I had a sister I would have eaten her.

No, I would have torn her out of a book and made her wear clothes I didn't want to wear. She would not have had a choice.

The idea for paper dolls came from cave drawings. They are petroglyphs that left their stationary position. It was not until after the invention of paper they could be cut from their surroundings. It was not until after the invention of scissors they could be cut. It was not until after the invention of metal that scissors could be made —

> An ancient Japanese purification ceremony dating back to at least A.D. 900 included a paper figure and a folded paper object resembling a kimono, which were put to sea in a boat. | Judy M. Johnson, *History of Paper Dolls*

Some excerpts from *The History of Paper Art Dolls*, by Aisling D'Art, in *Art Doll Quarterly*:

> Paper was invented in China around 105 C.E.
> The Original Paper Doll Artists Guild is based in Kingfield, Maine.

I plan my own article for the *Art Doll Quarterly*: Electric wired hair. Roto doll. Meta doll. I cut out text as though paper doll clothes. I write until the writing becomes photographs, and the photographs, the space in the album between the writing.

I make a paper doll who wore everything she had as did the Indians. A hide dress would last. It was all animal skin. A blanket if she was cold. Sometimes outerwear. Snow gear from the catalog. Battery-warmed mukluks. Some beads. Elk teeth.

I make a paper doll named, Lazarus, and name it, the thirst of a rich man — Luke 16:19–31.

Sometimes I made paper doll dresses of newspaper. I let the paper dolls wear stories I didn't want to hear. I used paper dolls to understand my placement in the world. Or lack of it. I moved the paper dolls in their imaginary lives making a way for my own life. How do I understand the world? How do I understand my place in it? By making paper dolls move. By placing clothes upon them. By having the power to clothe.

> The placement of figures
> The empty space around them
> The proportions— | Henri Matisse, *Notes of a Painter*

>> ...carrying the weight of that cumbersome box on legs which are cruelly positioned for walking. | Edward Hoagland, *The Courage of Turtles*

Once in a while I get this sense so brief I hardly know it—but a sense of some enormity that was or could have been. A way of life that has been so erased there are just streaks and those streaks hardly visible—but in them, a spot of grief and longing so overwhelming—

I hold up the dress as if it is for the missing sister.

Or the person I could have been had I had access to that other, lost life.

I had a sense of stability. A sense that it was a lie. I trained my paper dolls to walk in a fragmented text. I trained them to stand in open space. I showed them how to hop between the shifting subject matters.

This is just lacework, they will say. This is not writing, they will complain. It can't hold water. But I want a text like a paper-doll book.

I want a place for the mismatched, odd pieces that don't go together. I want fragments, bypasses, cutouts, splits, incomplete sentences, hanging clauses, disagreeing tenses. Starting a new, incomplete sentence when the previous incomplete sentence had not been finished. Or finalized. Thoughts moving ahead to other unrelated thoughts. The way I hear a power saw a few doors down and think of the carpenter, Jesus. The way I see the autumn trees handing out their leaves to the multitudes.

A paper doll is a road. A paper doll is travel. A paper doll is car repair. A paper doll is a fortress. A defense. A memory of school.

I learned self-determination from my paper dolls. I learned my placement in dichotomy. I made paper doll selves I would follow. They were costume. Disguise. Yet they were both disguise and a revealer of truth.

The paper dolls were my sisters. They were myself. They were a yearning for autonomy. They could never stand on their own without a prop.

Paper dolls were my first road dreams. I found travel and destination in them. Paper doll clothes were a geography of language.

What can I make from nothing? —As I travel the road wrapped in veils of grief. I have known failure and longing on the long roads I have driven. I have heard the turmoil of broken fields. I have been on the academic front where I served as a professor. I have longed to wrap students in my arms for their long struggles behind and ahead. I have been a *pray-er* for the world. I have driven long roads. Ignored. Dismissed. Yet I found autonomy for the broken.

I received an Equal Opportunity Fellowship to the Iowa Writer's Workshop with gratefulness to Gerald Stern. Alvin Greenberg hired me at Macalester College. Over the years, I had access to faith and writing and teaching. I had opportunity to find *place*, cracked and rough-edged as it was. I had the privilege of publication and promotion. I had access to the work that held my life together.

> Air is the worst enemy that paper dolls have. | Roma M. Welsh, *Early History of Paper Dolls*

The open air was all I had. I laid these words for pavement so I could walk across the air. These words must be pavement. I am walking on these words. These words I speak from air.

The Old Geography Lessons of Language

I am a sojourner as my fathers were. | Psalm 39:12

I wake with a dream from which I begin to write a journey. A black and white photo: a street, uphill, with rows of older, brick two-story houses facing one another, brownstones maybe they are called. There is snow on the street and up the steps to the front doors of heavy beveled glass. At the top of the street is a school, or a church, or both, Catholic, where Jesus bleeds on his cross. But my family was not Catholic. We did not have nuns, priests, catechism, and all the trappings. We did not live on that street. We were Protestants. We belonged to Trinity Methodist Church. I felt somewhat invisible, left out of Catholicism, yet fearful and dismissive of it at the same time.

Up the street, in my dream, children were stamped with religion. They wore uniforms. Nuns slapped their hands with rulers. Their mothers pushed out children and more children for pain and humiliation in front of others. They were washing and ironing hourly. Did I long for the burden of icon and imagery? The smell of incense? The unbearable weight of litany? The confession booth?

As Methodists, our high and remote priest was Christ. We believed no particular doctrine. We attended church, but church stayed in church. It barely made an impact in our lives other than an unexamined habit. Our church was a fortress-like Missouri limestone structure on Armour Boulevard in Kansas City, Missouri, where I had regular attendance, tucked away in the basement Sunday School classes.

Why did I dream of brick or brownstone houses crowded together, a church at the top of the street? No way out. Nowhere to go but up where I didn't belong. Houses like ones I never lived in. What I remember of my old neighborhood were the small houses along Woodland and 50th Terrace. What I saw in my dream were substantial brownstones. In my old neighborhood, our house sat at the top of the street. In my dream, there was a large school or church at the top of the street. The neighborhood in the photo in my dream was formalized, more established than my old neighborhood of bungalows. It was after all, a photo, a representation, maybe a misrepresentation of what I remember. Maybe I was reminded of the authority of the past, an authority that felt *papal*. There was a convent farther up the street on Woodland that might have further established that impression. My mother ran the house with order. Maybe the church or school was a representation of my house, a place that would mark or stamp my life, as far as feelings were concerned, with a Mother Superior at the head. Maybe my old neighborhood was transformed in the dream into brownstones with heavy doors, father priest, mother nun, nowhere to go but punishment in a cold atmosphere. Maybe that's what was couched in my winter dream.

My great-grandfather, Woods Lewis, was a fugitive, running from trouble in Indian Territory just before the Civil War. He fled to Tennessee, joined a cavalry regiment in the Union Army, and later settled in northwestern Arkansas because he couldn't return to Indian Territory, though he tried, but word got out. The exact trouble had several versions. He was a full-blood Cherokee. He did something that got him in trouble. He ran. Later he had eight children. One of them, I know, married into a religious family. She was my grandmother, bridging the renegade and the fundamentalists.

We used to play kickball in the street—on 50th Terrace that came up the hill from Paseo, where the street flattened for three or four houses before it reached Woodland Avenue where we lived. My father was a fugitive also—like his grandfather. He was fleeing poverty in northern Arkansas. He came to Kansas City just before the Depression and worked for the stockyards forty-six years before his death.

This is a ball kicked down the street: This dream piece. This piece dreamed with the sharp transitions of a dream. In the dark and murky journey forever on its way to truth—I write these words to make a place on which to stand.

I wonder what the neighborhood looked like before houses. North and south from our house on Woodland Avenue, the street rose in both directions. Houses on the streets behind us, to the east, continued to rise. Michigan. Euclid. Garfield. Brooklyn. It must have been a high ridge that Indians used to look out across Kansas City toward the Missouri River before it was Kansas City. It was on the other side of Francis Willard Elementary School at the top of the hill that the streets descended toward Prospect.

As a child, I was afraid the car would fall over backward as we came up the hill on 50th Terrace. I know fear was a part of my childhood. I was in a family that didn't seem to want to be together. If one member were voted out of the family, it would have been me. It seemed a regiment of terror, of wounding. It was all encompassing. I was the one coming up the hill in the car. I was the one playing kickball in the street. I was the ball rolling down the street. I was the game. It is true—I was the last one chosen to be on a team for kickball. I was the ball kicked down the steep hill into passing traffic on Paseo that would not stop for a ball. I was in a kickball game that included World War II, strike lines, rationing, the threat of polio. It was strict. It was uncomfortable. I had stitches and more stitches and scarlet fever and typhoid shots during the 1951 flood of the Kansas River that washed over the stockyards where my father worked. I stood vaccinated, tonsils removed, scared, scarred. My stick legs trembling before it all. And there were other fears of attack — eventually atomic bomb drills, squatting under our school desks with our arms over our heads.

Now the ball is kicked down the street again no one can catch it down the steep hill of 50th Terrace into the Paseo traffic where it got hit and hit, run over, smashed as I was in my school years, university years without voice or grounding. A sense of self-doubt and a general feeling of *unwantedness*. Lost. Hit. Hurt. A churl. Where do these words come from? I was decimated as a small kickball under the wheels of traffic. Did the cars laugh at their power over me? But Christ was there as the One: I am come to seek the lost and I would find the inflated kickball again. Kicked back up the street the way he could kick, and I rolled once again into the dream that both flattened and inflated the Christ who entered the darkness of my sleep with his dream. I was the game for whom Christ died.

Where did that faith come from? The deus ex machina? How suddenly did it happen? Why was Christ there? I knew it was him, whom others didn't seem to recognize, howbeit he was invisible. How could they? Why could some believe and others not? Was it choice, or realization, a knowing he was, a certainty? I believed because I had need, but others did and didn't believe. Was it because I was prone to the spirit world? But so are others and they find spiritualism of various kinds outside Christ. Why did it happen that way? Jesus was a shepherd and he wanted his sheep around him. That's why I have gone to church when I would rather have done other things. And why did it stick, overshadowing all? Look to me, and be saved, all the ends of the earth, for I am God, and there is none else — Isaiah 45:22. That for me has been truth.

In that dark chapter called *the lost the lost when I had no wings* I felt a presence there. It seems to me it was the *I am he who was and is* was there. There was nowhere else. The houses in the dream were close enough they were joined, no yards between not even fences to climb, but stumble through a darkness of sorts up a hill. The kicked ball now kicked again—

My mother was from a farm in Kansas, not in a town, but maybe ten miles from a town that hardly existed. A grocery store, a feed store. That was Prescott, Kansas. Was there a post office? Certainly not a bank. They had no money for the bank anyway. The bank was in Fort Scott, Kansas, or Hume, Missouri, still farther away. They lived along the state line of Missouri-Kansas. They were not interesting. They were known, lived with; they did not have the sharp division of my father's family. The edges of their struggle were suppressed. They had farmed in Missouri. They had farmed in Kansas. They were sturdy, enduring, surviving people. They knew poverty, mainly, and life on the land with its extremes of heat and cold and coming up with everything on their own. Their life was their own. No one decided for them. They kept themselves *uncluttered*.

I went to school in Kansas City, writing the letters of the alphabet, reading, learning arithmetic, geography, the states and their capitals, history, and recess. I remember the walk up the hill to school, crowded with bigger boys I was afraid of, or looked past, or kept my eyes to the ground, and one day, running across the street, I tripped on the curb, fell, and broke my permanent front tooth, which would have a tin band around it holding some sort of false corner on the tooth. Every time I smiled, there was the metal band around my front tooth.

What was meaningful in school? While the Catholic school, it seemed to me, from what I heard, was terrorizing its children with the threat of hell and the wilderness outside the Catholic Church, Francis Willard and other elementary schools across America were suffocating students with boredom, never giving anything in an interesting way. Making dishwater of learning. Where was something to which I could connect? Where were we going and why?

Where was something I could have a stake in? Where was learning I could own? And what was this Christian religion outside my school with its divisions and fractures? — Methodist, Catholic, and all the other denominations?

I remember seeing pictures of the young Queen Elizabeth visiting her kingdom, her colonial empire with her pocketbook and a small bouquet of flowers in her hands — in India her people were covered with mud, in Africa, dung, at the North Pole, ice. And blubber. In Denmark, reindeer. In Russia, there was a greater want than in my neighborhood. There was vodka to dull the rage. And over this, the war in heaven, and the God who could strike the earth with earthquake, or war or famine, and did many times, but always in other countries, though we had small disasters that dominated the newspapers from time to time, a child fallen into a mine shaft or a child kidnapped and murdered. Meanwhile there was our history with its code of rise and fall, upheaval and defeat, no matter who the army, the war for power. The inevitable move toward inflation. The expanding universe *overridden* with it. No matter who the commander. But we were not to worry about it in the Methodist Church. We weren't sure about the fires of hell. And some man trying to figure out why we were in church, finally came up with the idea that it was community. We were there to be with one another for a sense of togetherness on Sunday mornings. To be reminded of our Sunday School years as children. That over the freedom of our lives there was somewhere the idea of responsibility and a distant neighbor, God, who needed to hear from us. Our pennies in the collection plate, our attendance in church.

And somehow in my need and fear and suffering, Christ grabbed my shirt collar and took me to his office where he was the one beat.

Church was not catalyst back then. It was not change. It was not personal. It could be left behind as we piled in the car waiting for the roast that was in the oven, the mashed potatoes my mother would whip over the stove. My mother was in it for life. My father could go to work five mornings a week to whatever was out there in the stockyards. On Saturdays he used to go hunting. And I was left with a yearning for something I would later realize was called *art*, kept out of reach, not necessary for Depression-era parents who were practical to the core, not realizing the practicality of critical thinking, of dream, of art.

The same community I guess the man felt in church, but it never reached my family because of the idea that we were a family that went to church and had dinner on our plate every meal. And underneath, a desperate unhappiness that erupted in her volcanic anger, and the murmuring and erratic chatter and protest I heard on her deathbed as she talked out of her head for three days and nights before she died. It was an oppressive order. I suppose you didn't need the Catholic Church, or what I thought of it, anyway, to provide that. It was idealism. It was America who kept the rest of the nations in a dialogue bubble. Not letting onto the page anything other than what the author of the world, America, allowed.

After all it was the land where I first tasted freedom. On my maternal grandfather's farm where I could explore the cellar, the barn, the roof of the pig shed, the fields, the windbreak, the pond. It was outside where I played though the wind nearly swept me from the ground. It was the trips from the city to the farm, maybe once a month. I don't remember going to church there. We stayed on the farm on Sunday mornings. My grandparent's church was the Hume Methodist Church in Hume, Missouri, though they lived in Kansas. The Hume church was where their funerals were held. It was the only time I was there. They all are buried in the Hume, Missouri, cemetery—the Woods and Adamses.

Back to Kansas City with the bell of the Catholic church clanging over the neighborhood, though it was actually the bell from the convent farther up the hill on Woodland Avenue—and we ran from it as the religion that robbed its people of their freedom other than to turn out more Catholics. That seemed to be the major plan. So they could take over the world. So there would be a one-world religion. Who knows where the Muslims were. They were rarely thought of in the fifties.

Where do these ideas come from?

I knew how fundamentally divided the Christian faith was, and then there were the Jews, a few of them, in school. And now the militant, fundamental Black Muslims with a new chant to bring down America like a kickball kicked down the street.

I remember exotic photographs of Africa and Egypt in the National Geographic. My mother's friend, Thelma Keiser, who never married, traveled to Alaska sending back photographs of herself standing by an Eskimo man. And my father saying, that's what would have happened to my mother without him, as she stirred potatoes, and what would be wrong with that? Not having a man, a family, to be on the outskirts, wearing a plane ticket for a heart and a decal from faraway places on your luggage. A life of travel of freedom. A house of my own. A job of my own. A geography of my own words. When I was a child in Kansas City, I played with a girl up the street who had a play kitchen under the back porch of her house. I liked it there in that place of her own, though it groomed or geared us toward making meals. Our very play was in serving.

It was in a wood-paneled room at Francis Willard Elementary School where I first saw a parking lot, or a port, so to speak. I was in fifth grade. It had to do with a sewing room, a costume room maybe for a school play, but I had been left out of that too. I was in the background. But I got to see the creative room, I got to stand there as if only a moment before my father was transferred from Kansas City to Indiana.

In Indianapolis, Mrs. Timmons was waiting. She was my sixth grade grammar teacher and she did not like me. I don't know how I knew this, but I knew. I was at Flackville grade school a year and a half before my father was transferred to St. Louis. I started my first day of seventh grade while we were living in a hotel in downtown St. Louis. But soon we had our house and I entered my high school years in St. Louis.

Last summer, I visited Trinity Methodist Church, where I had gone as a child. The usual story. The church to me had been huge, disproportionate — the smaller the child, the larger the space it is in. The stained-glass windows were still there: four of the apostles, Matthew, Mark, Luke, John in one window. Abraham, Moses, Hosea, and Isaiah in another. Hosea? In a stained glass window with a green-faced, horned serpent, an image of Satan with a green glove of a face?

Of Hosea I know:

>Hosea 4:6 — My people are destroyed for the lack of knowledge.
>Hosea 6:1 — Let us return to Jehovah. He has torn. He will heal.

Once I lived in a house up a hill. It stood at the head of the street as the church did in my dream. The house at the top of the hill so steep you couldn't see the house until you climbed the hill. My way away from there: Write and then get up and read what you wrote. Make your way with what you've done. Stand on the geography you've made with your writing, your words.

In *The American Poetry Review*, September/October 2002, Barbara Guest wrote a piece called "Wounded Joy." She says, "Do you notice as you write that no matter what there is on the written page something appears to be in back of everything that is said, a little ghost[?]" She goes on to talk about a *more*, an *elsewhere*, a *hiddenness*. Guest is talking about poetry, but she also is talking about the dream. It seems to me our dreams struggle to *out* the *hider*, to reveal the one hiding, as poetry seeks to unreel the same territory. It seems to me, the dream struggles to kick the ball up the street.

A dream confronts the confrontation of ghosts. A dream itself is a ghost confronting other ghosts in the process of the confrontation.

There is texture; a written geography of language as conduit. A dream redistributes the distributions after the conquest of waking. Once again, the conscious thought recovers from its slippage into the oblivion of sleep. A dream bypasses the ear, the old receptacle of story in oral tradition. Yet the always previous territory is there, ghosting or *spiritizing* or *abstracting* the soundless written text of the dream, the visual imagery of its words or pictographs.

Maker — Begetter — because you are forever: provide, forgive, deliver —

A dream is a language aligned to the movement of the sky. On earth as it is in heaven.

A dream requires a dream language in which to speak.

A dream itself is a displacement / a sojourner / a kicked ball.

Truth invents history. It adds what has been left out. There is the truth of what I saw in the past and the truth of what I felt. There is the truth of the way I remember the past — The way it was, or the part of it I chose to relate to — The part meaningful to me would not be the part meaningful to my brother or father or mother. A dream presents the feelings of the past.

The neighborhood of brownstone houses I saw in the dream was a photograph, a black and white photograph, and not the actual neighborhood. My mind was a camera taking a picture of the emotional world I lived in. The photo was the feelings of the past. The truth presented in a dream. The telling of the other versions, all versions of all events, to the winnowing basket to be winnowed. A composite that history always is. Bringing into perception what is to be known, the invisible other world, the ways in which to see it — this is the way to look at it, and this is the way to look at it. I taught the left-out history for years, the Native American perspective, and I learned also the left-out parts of my life.

The truth of versions; the versions of truth or truths in the folds or crevices of a dream. A dream invents the geography of its language because it needs imagination to enfold it — a language or topography of dream-thinking. If ever there was a non-fit — an un-fit — it is language and the meaning it has to carry.

A dream does not have one definition, but it is a guide, a messenger, a prophet, a presenter of more-than-one-way- to-see. A dream is what is left at the end of the day. It is reruns. It is a leaf pile. The dream is a measuring rod. A parochial neighborhood: an idealistic setting, substantial houses, a neighborhood, a church at top. Family. Community. God. Three prongs of our existence. Which interpretation do I chose to interpret the interpretations of the dream?

Now the ball kicked another way. Now another change in direction:

Drive away from the small child on Woodland at 50th Terrace in Kansas City, my father in the stockyards in the river bottoms at the confluence of the Kansas and Missouri Rivers. The streets of the stockyards: Genesee, Wyoming, Union. The stockyards razed. The streets deserted.

A marriage past, a son and daughter wounded from the split, the quiet wrongdoing, the guilt, the guilt, that I opened them up to pain. Introduced them to the kicked ball, the decline after the flat part of the street into the traffic on Paseo below.

How do I face fundamental religion? With its often mindlessness? With its *fracturings*. Jesus is Lord. I was born in sin in a fallen world. I am acceptable to God by belief in the shed blood of Christ for the propitiation of my sins. He is my intercessor. My interceder. Why does an intellectual suppression have to come with it? Going to an evangelical church while being a professor at a small liberal arts college is another form of loneliness, but all things are possible.

I have a Muslim colleague who talks about the ultimate placement as state. For the Christian, it is a person, Jesus Christ, at least for the kind of Christian I am, the Protestant Martin Luther Wittenberg-door's *the just shall live by faith*—Hebrews 18:38. Most other colleagues speak of no God at all. In my surface perusal, anyway—these thoughts and memories to get through. What a riptide we inhabit.

Last summer after visiting Trinity Methodist Church, I visited several other churches in Kansas City, looking for a church to attend when I leave Minnesota. I heard various sermons, some of them gaudy, argumentative, pleasant, boring, broken, sometimes wrongful, it seemed to me. One of them was about re-envisioning God, for which I have minimal tolerance. The minister, a woman, talked about the need for re-envisioning God in the years after the Holocaust. How could the God we knew before Hitler's Germany be the God we know afterward? I don't think God has to explain himself to us. I think he's wrapped in a mystery we can't understand. He does what he wants to do. He allows what he allows. I think it says within the text of the Bible that there are wars in heaven—spiritual forces against spiritual forces. Maybe the evil *forces* knew that God favored the Jews. Maybe that's why they were the recipient of the atrocities during World War II. Maybe the evil forces tried to shut down history by trying to so anger God that he would end the world before it could run its course. Did not God destroy once by Noah's flood? Maybe anything I say about it is stupid. Who knows why the Holocaust happened, other than the evil that is in the heart of man? We are the makers of history. We are the instigators of the evil intent. The series of events called history is run by the machine of the human will. Is it not happening on various scales throughout the world? What is in us that required the death of the Son of God on the cross to alleviate? In that event, God judged the world in the person of Jesus Christ. Whoever believes in the cross bypasses the judgment of death on the world of unbelievers—those not covered by faith in the blood of Jesus. How can anyone believe that?

The Christians believe—or some Christians do—that there are forces that cannot be appeased, such as Hitler, and possibly terrorists. It seems to me that war sometimes is necessary. I was a small child when Japan attacked a U.S. fleet in Pearl Harbor. America retaliated by invading Japan with a bomb, and because they did not surrender, another bomb was dropped three days later. When al-Qaeda invaded New York City and Washington, D.C., America went after Saddam instead of Osama. We invaded a country that was not directly involved and avoided the ones that were. War is profitable to those making the war machines. The war clothes. It gives the military something to do. God and war. War and God. The usual anger and dismay at the unclarity of direction. The mish-mash we wade through as nation, as a world—into which I wake in a neighborhood still in a dream where I am a stranger, other than I know the city and the fall and rising of its streets.

The Girl Made of Cotton Grass

There's a story I found in *The Eskimo Storyteller*, edited by Edwin S. Hall Jr., about a boy who saw a girl dressed in mukluks and parka. *aanii, aanii, these are my clothes,* she said. When he looked again, she was gone. He saw only cotton grass.

It's a story about mirage and the effects of light on the atmosphere of the Arctic. The moving grasses turned into the perception of a parka and mukluks. I liked the story because often I felt haunted by jabs from the past that were no longer there. But in certain light, I could see more than what is there. Old paper dresses become transparent. I take the parka from my closet. The sun shines white on an ice field. Or is it paper? Or the cotton grass moving on the tundra of my room?

Tell me it is not so. That I have overlooked something that I should know. That I am less than I could have been.

Where did the transformer come from? The prayers were not in my house. Not in school. Maybe they were in Sunday school and church after all. Maybe I heard them in my head. In the scrump of mukluks on the crusty snow. Is it you, Lord, on the other side? I cannot see, but feel someone there.

Mukluk

I am haunted by the terrorism of the past. I make ordinary statements to bypass—
    I am glad Jefferson City is the capital of Missouri.
    I am glad Topeka is the capital of Kansas.
    I came to the edge of myself over which there was a drop. I had to hang on. I had to grip with my mukluks. Hold tight to my parka. Again, I would have a place in the cotton grass.
    These are my clothes. *aanii. aanii.* These are my clothes.
    She opened me up and poured in the poison. The self-doubt, the self-destruction. The polio of emotional crippling. Here let me pat you. This is going to hurt you, but I will first make it feel good. In those childhood days when I had no way out. No escape but the corner vacant lots. Nowhere to turn but to be her burden. When no one would come to help. When no one knew what was happening. The fire when I saw it coming. The snake when it began to move in the quiet room and I knew it would strike no matter how still or invisibly I stood. When I would have to go on as though normal. The hurt showed. A turtle in a shell of fear. It is the history of clothing.
    A mukluk is a boot worn by Eskimos. Mukluk is a Yupik word meaning "bearded seal." Though mukluks were sometimes made of reindeer skin. In the Utqiaguik Collection in the Inupiat Cultural Center in Barrow, Alaska, there is a mukluk estimated to be between three hundred to five hundred years old.

It is because of the words I hang upon myself that I am clothed.

There has been war. There still is war everywhere. Yet I'm playing with paper dolls. Beware. Don't be misled. Do not underestimate. There was something that pushed outward, that connected with something far away. Somehow, in the underbrush, I knew I was alone with the world. And with history to some extent. I am talking about paper dolls, but underneath, it is Ou'Wash.

Who is Ou'Wash? Where does Ou'Wash come from? The skull cellars of the world—World War II Germany that haunted my childhood. The trips to Union Station in Kansas City where the soldiers left. In Asia, Pol Pot comes to mind. Mao Tse-tung, in my lifetime, killed seventy million Chinese by starvation and outright murder. The Gulags of Russia. Bosnia/ethnic cleansings. Darfur, Sudan. All those starving in Niger, Africa—those children paper thin/one dimensional. Regimes in Iraq/Iran. South America/Pinochet. Israel/Palestine. Al Qaeda/Hezbollah/terrorists. Native Americans hunted down and banished to reservations. The names that wrap the world in butcher paper. This is only a few. And to some minor degree—the mother cooking on the home front—on the frontline of the stove. The row of flames that engulfed us. The frightening core of the human will. I knew the history of the world was war. I picked it up in my family. I had an uncle in the war with Germany. My father's history was one of removal. Of relocation. Of an unexplained loss. Therefore, there had to be something else there—The faith of a paper doll dress.

Holocaust

Though we made burnt offerings of our children.

He's here — Ou'Wash. The terrorism will not go away. Destroy. Destroy, I hear him say.

In the book of Job in the Old Testament, there was a day when Satan came before the Lord, and the Lord said, see my servant — Job 1:6? Satan said, yes, but you have a screen around him. You have *bubbled* him. Let me have him and see what he says. Do what you want, God said, but spare his life. So Satan tried Job. His cattle were stolen, his children died, his wife nagged. Sores covered his body. His friends accused him of sin. He was being punished for some wrongdoing. What was it, Job? They asked. Speak up.

Satan said to God, you like Jews, do you? Give them to me and see what happens. I'll muddy the fields. I'll make a swamp for anyone who believes.

Then Satan tempted God with unspeakable events. For a moment, Satan saw if he could run things. Burn the whole lot with ovens. Show what one man can do to another.

They would have kept coming until the whole was wholly burned.

Roads, bridges, using force to stomple force.

An army infected with dissent, a divided country with atrocities in its borders. *Ou'Wash* — the voices from the skull pockets speak.

Someone caustic at those talks on campus I have to go to says America entered World War II to save Jews, but underneath it was to smash European power. No, we can't have human suffering to that extent. Yes, we have to come out on top of the pile.

A Book of Roads

The earth seems to me a book of roads. Maybe because of all the movings I have done. It seems to me the road holds voices. It holds meaning. Memory. Story. Discovery. I find notes left over from travel: *The late October trees, red; the sky, mauve; the underclouds, a brownish, rust red.* I like the migratory aspect of travel, the spatial positioning. I see the passing earth by the geography of its language. *A duck flaps its wings to get over the interstate, maybe to a nearby marshland or wetland, not graceful, not soaring hawklike over the road.* Always in the Midwest, there are long streaks across the sky where planes cross.

My road trips began as a child. My mother's parents lived on a Kansas farm seventy miles south of Kansas City, Missouri. I don't remember exactly how many times we traveled there, but according to the photos in my mother's old album, it was often. I got used to *going*. My father's mother was in Arkansas. We did not travel there as much.

On the road, because I have done it so often, there is a sense of purpose, of destination, of task, of achievement. I am cut off from small duties. I am connected to larger ones: thought, endurance, survival. There is a heightened *sense of being* when I am on the road. My usual trips are weekly: St. Paul to Kansas City to my family, 439 miles, seven hours. A stop in Des Moines for gas and two short rest stops.

Driving the land by myself has become part of my writing process. It is in passing over land that I come to *know*. These are not the short journeys, but the long ones covering miles and miles. On this trip I am driving from St. Paul, Minnesota, to the Oregon coast and then to Texas. A journey of nearly six thousand miles. Those are the journeys I am talking about, mile after mile on the prairie.

Frederick Buechner, Christian philosopher, wrote in his book *On the Road with the Archangel*, "Religion points to that area of human experience where in one way or another man comes upon mystery as a summons to pilgrimage." Or, maybe it is in the mileage over passing land that I find the summons to mystery. I would say it is what I have felt in the pilgrimage of travel. It is when I am alone on the road that religion often appears to me.

For the Native American, stories were embedded in journey. The journey or migration usually was followed by teepee-drawings depicting experiences during the journey. Now a journal replaces the drawings.

The sun will not smite you (Isaiah 49:10) was the verse I started with on the long trip — Minnesota to Texas by the way of the Oregon coast — comforting since I was going to make a long, circular journey that included a drive through the Nevada desert on my way to Texas. Amusing also, because on June 24 when I left, I passed through a downpour west of Minneapolis on I-94 around 7:00 a.m. I wrote: *lightning, thunder, downpour, miles of incoming traffic, water across the road in low places, thunder, lightning, a lighter sky, windshield wipers down a notch. Open sky. Open road.*

I have several purposes for the trip: continued research on "Stone Heart," a book for the bicentennial of the Lewis and Clark expedition, from the Native American perspective. I have a conference in Oregon, and a trip to a family gathering — a wedding in Texas. The previous summer I had driven along the Missouri and Columbia Rivers but had not been through the Bitterroot

Mountains in Idaho, especially the two mountain passes, Lemhi and Lolo, where Lewis and Clark nearly starved and froze to death in the late autumn of 1805.

Lemhi Pass in Idaho is on a single-lane dirt road that climbs through the pines to just over seven thousand feet before it descends. I had a box of books to take to the conference, a large suitcase for the twenty days I would be gone, a small bag to carry into the motel at night. I even had my grandson's car seat in the backseat my daughter had given me the last time I was in Kansas City so they wouldn't have to carry it to the wedding in Texas on the plane. I also travel with a file box where I keep projects on which I'm working, another box of maps and tablets of paper and books on tape such as the Bible, a tape on Jewish history, one on Islam, and the Journals of Lewis and Clark. Of course, I had my laptop and portable printer. A large purse. Hanging clothes for the wedding. Shoes and assorted other articles. A few rocks and pine cones I picked up along the way. All this I took up the hairpin curves and dust of the dirt road to Lemhi Pass, my ears popping in the altitude, my car continuing to climb.

My car had 65,161 miles on the odometer when I left on June 24. It had 71,110 miles when I returned on July 13. The car was a box of books lighter. But basically everything returned with me in good order. I even forgot to leave the car seat at my daughter's when I passed through Kansas City on I-35 on my way back from Texas to Minnesota. But I would be returning the next weekend. That is one of the shorter trips.

After Oregon, I drive to Texas, south through northern California into Nevada because I want to see Walker Lake and Grant Mountain where the Ghost Dance began, a phenomenon among Native Americans in the late nineteenth century. When I write about something, I have to be on the land where the story happened. I pick up the setting and a sense of the story. Land informs the piece. How can we sing the Lord's song in a strange land—Psalm

137:4? How can I write words that don't connect to the land? I think the land somehow carries the voices that have passed there, or some vestige of them. It's where I get the words I write. As I am finishing one project, I like to start another. Or several others. This new project is about the Ghost Dance, the Messianic dances that took place among the Native Americans when they realized their way of life was coming to an end. No one knows what happened, but after reading an account by Kicking Bear, it seems like there was divine intervention, or some sort of revival, to prepare the Indians for what was ahead. Did Christ appear in America to the Indians in visions and dreams during the Ghost Dances from 1888 to 1890? Does anything like that happen any longer? Did nothing happen and it only seemed like something? It was an issue I wanted to pursue.

    I picked up a rock from Walker Lake, made some notes, which became the beginning of "The Dance Partner." From Nevada, I crossed into Arizona at Hoover Dam. Ahead, there was a checkpoint before the drive across the dam. There was a line of cars and a long wait. Maybe it was slow because it was tourist season. Maybe it was the aftermath of 9-11, cars pulled off to the side, trunks open. Then I drove across Arizona and into New Mexico, where I stayed a night in Gallup. The next day I continued to Texas. My son now lives in Rhome, which is about twenty miles northwest of Fort Worth. Those three days I drove from Oregon to Texas, all that way through the Nevada desert and the Southwest, there was cloud cover. So there was the promise. It was still hot. And there was sun from time to time. But there was cloud cover and the sun did not *smite* me.

    I listened to the Psalms as I traveled—they rolled by as a moving landscape—taken out of their numbered order, though I know that each verse has its place within the Psalm, and that each Psalm has its place within the Psalms, and that the book of Psalms has its place among the other books in the Old Testament. But listening while driving, instead of reading in a chair in my room, the Psalms travel the road.

> A stunting of Psalm 136:
> to him who paved the earth above the waters
> to him who made the sun to rule the day
> the moon the stars to rule the night
> who struck Egypt in their firstborn
> and brought Israel out from among them
> who divided the Red Sea
> and made Israel pass through
> but overthrew Pharaoh and his army
> to him who led his people through the wilderness
> who slew kings and gave their land for a heritage.

Who is this God? I still ask. It is the same God that some of the people believed who came to this country and displaced the native tribes. I hear his voice in the migration across the land, maybe the same way my ancestors knew the Maker in their movement across the land, only now I call his name, Christ. Migration was not only to get from one place to another, summer to winter camp, or following buffalo herds during the hunt, but migration was a process for the development of oneself as a human being—for knowing one's relationship to the larger, spiritual realm, and the Maker. In travel, I know God is larger than our human understanding of him. I long to reach that place.

I like to be on the road by myself, for a while anyway. I want to do it because I can. My family is raised. I am alone. I want to do it while I *still* can. Besides, I couldn't figure out any other way to get everywhere I had to go with everything I needed to take. There wasn't time to go one place, fly back home, fly to another place. Research was part of the trip also.

These are the times drawn into myself. To see what anguish. Abandonment. Aloneness is there.

I worried about my ability to drive day after day without anyone to talk to, with the loneliness of traveling alone (though I like it, as I said), of having the responsibility of deciding where to eat, where to sleep, where to stop for gas. I remember buying gas and passing the next station where it was ten cents a gallon cheaper. Often I have the ability to stop at the highest prices for gas. I remember driving in Montana and looking at my gas tank and seeing it nearly on empty and how did I let that happen where gas stations are far apart? Fortunately I made it to Billings, though I couldn't have gone much farther. I remember the motels by the train tracks I didn't notice when I checked in. The motels with thin walls and creaking doors when I was trying to sleep.

On the trip, I listened to another tape, "The Gift of the Jews, How a Tribe of Desert Nomads Changed the Way Everyone Thinks and Feels," by Thomas Cahill. Our values, ethics, ideas, our Western civilization, itself, came from the Jews. The Jews broke cyclic thinking. All things became possible: history, the individual, even the concept of time itself. The history of the Jews is the story of God breaking into the human consciousness. We see the change from gods made with human attributes to humanity made in God's image.

I returned to tapes of the Bible. This one from Esther: Once there was a Jew, Mordecai, who would not bow to Haman, an officer of King Ahasuerus. Haman decreed Mordecai should be hanged and all Jews killed on such and such a day because he would not bow. The king signed the proclamation and dispatchers rode their horses, camels, mules, to the 127 provinces of Persia from Indian to Ethiopia saying to destroy, to slay, to cause to perish, all Jews. One night the king could not sleep. The Chronicles were brought to him. He discovered Mordecai had once told him of an assassination plot. Mordecai had not been rewarded. What should be done? King Ahasuerus asked Haman. Haman, thinking he was the one of whom Ahasuerus spoke, said, of course he should be honored. Meanwhile, Esther, the queen, also a Jew, which Ahasuerus apparently did not know, told the king his proclamation to kill all Jews included herself and Mordecai. The king could not rescind a proclamation he had signed, but he sent his dispatchers on horses, camels, mules, to the 127 provinces saying the Jews could defend themselves on such and such a day. Esther then asked that Mordecai be hanged. In fact, there already was a gallows, and Haman and his tens sons were hanged on the gallows Haman had made for Mordecai.

I imagined the ensuing battle in the Book of Esther as a teepee-hide drawing. I also thought of the book of Esther as a forerunner of the Holocaust.

It is in the private time on the road that I return to myself. Often, it is a time to envision. A time to see in the light of the road. A time in which I pick up the rhythms of writing. The long stretches of development. A departure toward a destination. Passage. Release. Driving on the road, I return to those times in the woods when I played as a child. On the road, I often have watched the hawks with their wings outspread, gliding on the air currents that rise from passing traffic. *A flock of birds over the road shifting direction: a black moth-eaten blanket shaken out.* I remember the sunflower fields in North Dakota. The sloughs. The bending grasses. The land is a road show.

These are my clothes. *aanii aanii.* These are my clothes.

Christianity began with a Diaspora, an outward movement from its center. By the time John wrote the book of Revelation, he was writing to seven churches all with different understandings and practices of Christianity. By the third century AD Constantine had conquered Rome and made Christianity the official religion and bound it to the state or empire. This was the rise of the Catholic Church, which remained until Martin Luther nailed his thesis to the Wittenberg door in 1517 proclaiming, "The Just Shall Live by Faith." Luther broke Christianity into Catholic and Protestant. The Protestant tried to return to the New Testament roots — a sense of personal commitment to Christ without a priest — but it resulted in a range of believers united mainly by their disagreements on the interpretation of the scripture. Since the Reformation, there has been further splintering of the splintered. Further denominations within denominations. Christianity also has its brutal history of Crusades, Holy Wars, Inquisitions, and the burning of heretics that it should acknowledge, as America should hear the voices from its history.

I always have wanted to see things I had not seen. To know what I did not know. To travel further than I had traveled. I asked for the road. I asked for the old migration trails. A colleague of mine from the East Coast says the driving I do must be different from the driving she is used to. She dreads driving on the crowded roads. But my driving usually is by choice and it is on the open roads of the straight interstates. Driving in traffic at rush hour is not the road travel I'm talking about, nor the single-lane, slow and winding roads of New England.

Returning to Minnesota from the long trip, I drove north through Texas and Oklahoma. It was good to see the red soil again, the red ponds. As I passed through Oklahoma City, there was a terrible rainstorm. At times, I hardly could see the road, but I knew where I-35 turned right and where it veered left. Then I continued north through the flint hills of Kansas into Missouri, staying a night with my daughter and her family in Kansas City before continuing through Iowa back to Minnesota.

I listened to a tape about Islam, a religion based not on individual redemption from sin in the person of Jesus Christ but on an egalitarian state established on the idea of a social justice of sorts. I don't know what the religion does about the innate sin evident in ourselves and in our histories. Mutilation, torture, and death of the transgressors or dissidents, I suppose. For some, Islam seems willing to betray the principles of peace stated in the Koran, and resort to violence to establish their state — their regime — after which will be the enforced peace. Christianity has that violence in its history also. I feel the same inherent contradictions and the coercion/non-coercion of Islam. There is something about the *sameness* for everyone that bothers me. The sameness of everyone. Would I be able to travel on my own if I were a Muslim woman in an Islamic state?

The only problem on the whole trip was inside the Minnesota border when I filled the car with gas one last time but couldn't find my wallet. I take care of my wallet when I travel. Money, credit card, and a photo ID are a lifeline when you are miles from anyone you know. You are nothing without them. It's what people want from you. It makes the travel happen. I took everything out of my large purse, my file box of maps, and books on tape I carry in the front seat on the rider's side. I looked under both front seats. I had paid for gas in Bethany, Missouri; I was sure I put the wallet back in my purse. I had stopped at a rest stop in Iowa. Had I forgot to lock the door? Did someone reach inside and take it? No, I was sure I had locked the doors. I couldn't figure out what had happened. I went through everything again. No wallet. I went inside with my checkbook. The clerk wouldn't take my check. Someone would have to come and pay. I didn't know anyone who would drive a hundred miles from St. Paul to pay for my gas. I asked to see the manager. He would only take a check if I had a photo ID. I said, it's in the wallet I can't find. We talked a long time. They had gotten too many bad checks. My check was not bad, I said. I had nowhere to turn. He finally made a call to my bank, and said he would take my check. As I got in the front seat of the car, the seat pulled away a little from the console, and I saw where my wallet had fallen. I don't know how it got there. As I said, I always take care to put it back into my large purse, which is always on the floorboard in the front seat. I went back inside and told the clerk I could pay cash since I'd found my wallet, but she only wanted to write my driver's license number on the check I had given her. To not be able to find your money must be what it feels like to live without faith.

Now I'm listening to Ottmar Liebert's *Nouveau Flamenco* and the beat of the old Creedence Clearwater Revival to cover the last stretch of road. I begin in silence. The middle passage is the books on tape. The end is the noise on which I rely.

This particular trip was finished, yet there would be other long ways to go.

In the volume of the book it is written — Psalm 40:7
Are my wanderings not in a book? — Psalm 56:8
A book of the records of the fathers — Ezra 4:15
A book of records of the chronicles — Esther 6:1
A book of remembrance — Malachi 3:16
A book of the road.

Book Two
Geographies of a Realigned Language

Native American Literature,
Issues, Ou'Wash, and Creative Theory

Sometime or other I think I ought to write an essay about the dreadful treatment given the Indians. If I ever get around to it, I'm hoping that somebody, someday, will write something that outlines the patriotism of those Indian chiefs who were only trying to save their own country from exploitation by the whites, who made treaties with the Indians and broke them every time they made one ... There were Indian tribes on the East Coast and in central New York — the Iroquois, for example, and the Algonquins ... who were working toward an organization that, in the long run, would have made them great statesmen and a great asset to our country if they'd been treated fairly. | Harry S. Truman, *Where the Buck Stops*

Instead of opening up the paper to a potential dialogue with Indian people whose experiences may have matched [Pratt's] expectations and desires ... he sought total control over the newspaper's narrative by inventing Indian voices — "paper Indians" who would speak nothing but the school's mythological narrative and reinforce disciplinary power without question. | Amelia V. Katanski, *Learning to Write "Indian"*

Flatland

> I will be assembled out of
> noisy ecru tissue paper
> printed with navy blue directions. | Caroline Knox,
> "Dress Pattern with an Interior," from *Quaker Guns*

At the Flatland Gallery in Minneapolis, I saw a [*domestica*] exhibit with an ironing board, washing machine, and various patterns for clothing. I remember those tissue-thin patterns the color of camels. Patterns pinned to cloth. To be cut out with pinking shears. Oh yes — Clothing as dialogue. Clothing as words. Our words as clothing. Our words as disguise.

Our clothing as ghosts.

Our dialogue cut apart with scissors.

Any of the many-dimensional possibilities in the concept of representation, especially in concert with the tension of a two-dimensional doll.

Our words as patterns for thought — in the [*domestica*] exhibit there was a voice sharp as a straight pin. These patterns I use as thoughts. Cutting out my own clothes. Cutting out my paper dolls and their paper clothes. And how do I iron a paper doll dress?

While reviewing the work of a colleague this past summer, I saw a drawing by Jaune Quick-to-See Smith called "Paper Dolls for a Post-Colonial World" in which there were two Native American paper dolls with various costumes with the usual tabs over the shoulders and down the sides — a blanket, a smallpox suit, a priest's robe, a voyageur outfit, a schoolboy outfit, and a garb that looked like a blackjack dealer. Smith also drew "Coyote Paper Dolls" with a camouflage suit among others, a hole cut out for coyote's tail. She used the idea or theme of disguise in connection with cultural commentary on the different costumes the Native American wears for assimilation.

There also is the point of having several *selves* to divert attack against *self*, to protect the core of self. The purpose of disguise: become another or others so the real self survives. I played with the persona of paper dolls to divert the wounding of the self I carried within me. I hear their voices again like straight pins.

I see the stars as clothes for the sky.

I see the struggle toward a native theory. Its definition.

Is it possible to use a *cross-genre* method to get at the gist of what I need to say to explain a cultural stance? I think of the cotton grass story since the point of the myth is the lack of boundaries in an interconnected world. Is it possible to change shapes or take on the attributes or properties of another?

I think of the late-1880s photograph of Wewha, a male Zuni potter dressed in women's clothes posing with his pottery. I saw the photograph and one of his pots in the Southwest Museum in Los Angeles.

I think of No Ear, who drew a Dakota winter count that has no pictographs when the definition of a winter count is pictographs of each year's main event. Among his text of events in consecutive years: *A Kiowa's skull was crushed. They brought curly horses. Man with red robe killed. Shooting Pine was captured. They swam toward a buffalo. Place of winter camp forgotten. Dogs also snow-blind.* No Ear's is the only winter count of words or *word marks* among the pictographs of American Horse, Battiste Good, Cloud Shield, Long Soldier, and the many others who drew winter counts on buffalo hides.

In the *American Poetry Review*, November/December 2005, Tzvetan Todorov asked, what remains of poetry if verse is removed? I would ask, what remains of any form of writing if the structure is disrupted? But it is in that disruption that often the *matter* of what I want to say is there. In the disrupted syntax of a sentence, even, I see what I want to say. It is there in that misconstruction. I feel it necessary from time to time — the fracturing of thought, the ready shifts and swift change in direction. Made-up words and a company of associations. The reverse side of the woven fabric draws me. The work of getting there. The two-dimensional flatland of teaching/scholarship and domesticity. Both have their *waverings* into tangents of explaining one's life — *explainings* that change forms — that cotton grass that is the sense of what it is to be — Therefore, a fragmentary, torn person can achieve the feeling of presence in whatever shape — because of that transformation in the cotton grass — it is what it is *to be*. I often feel the journeyings — the invisible mark lines on the earth. They are something that can't be gotten directly at. But in the dissociative fragmentation and indirectness, the essence is uncovered in its brokenness. The toe-line of a schedule. The surreal and subconscious dreams crossing into the waking. The integration of all that doesn't go together.

Soldiers as Paper Dolls

The news from history is difficult. I read it to my paper dolls.

> Some of the news I spare them.
> The Seventh Cavalry. The World Wars.
> Vietnam. Iraq.
> The threat of unrest in the near and middle east.
> Now they are dressed in camouflage to take the oil fields.

Minneapolis to Chicago to Frankfurt to Munich to Izmir. Twenty-two hours.

On a flight to Turkey, I sit next to a man who works for Haliburton during the war on Iraq. He is returning to Kuwait after his mother's funeral. He was in the Army during Desert Storm. But he's no longer a soldier, he says. He lives in a fenced camp and is taken by bus to work then returned to camp. Yes, it's a burden to be there. They are killing one another. But if we leave it will be worse — the ones that come after will be worse than the ones we got rid of.

The darkness brings with it a semisleep — images jut in front of one another — war trains out of place. Flying camouflage uniforms sitting up, unable to lie down. Unrelated yet somehow interconnected.

Hours later, the cabin lights go on. An announcement is made. The early sun comes in the window once the plane reaches light when my mouth is open and dry. We eat. We land.

SOLDIERS AS PAPER DOLLS

The Haliburton man waves to me as he leaves in another direction.

A guide and driver meet me at the airport in Izmir. I am stamped—approved to enter the country. They drop me off at the hotel where I lie flat on the bed.

The next morning we travel to the places I have come to research. I take the notes I have come to take. There are poplars and cypress on the winding roads above the Aegean. Minarets spike the small towns we pass. The road so rough sometimes I cannot write.

I see an American flag upside down on its post like a paper doll dress. I don't speak when we eat in restaurants. I don't want them to see I'm an American, though it shows, the guide says.

Afterward, I fly from Izmir to Istanbul to Tel Aviv. The next day I meet a colleague who is an anthropologist working there. The only American, he says. My purse is checked when we enter a restaurant. They are afraid of sidewalk bombs. I imagine eating, thinking any moment there could be an explosion.

The colleague takes me to the historical site of an ancient city. I get the feel of the sea. The incoming wind. The sound of birds. I dream of what could have been nearly two thousand years ago, finding voices on the land.

That night, in the *International Herald Tribune*, I read a story from the Rafah refugee camp on the Gaza Strip. During a four-day incursion, Israeli tanks pushed through the Rafah zoo. They knocked down trees and made big piles of earth with *a bulldozer that looked as if it had number 7 on the side. Then bulldozer No. 7 was joined by bulldozer No. 4.* They left a *moonscape* of twisted cages. The Israeli forces pushed through the zoo because they thought the main route was blocked by charges laid by Palestinians. The Israelis were trying to stop arms smuggled in from neighboring Egypt.

Out of eighty animals, only seven, including a wounded raccoon and a small kangaroo bounding around, remained—ducks and an ostrich were dead. Rather than leave the animals caged in a combat zone, the Israelis released them. The caged animals were now free to run wild in their terror across gunfire and crossfire. They were free to eat bullets.

Where were the others? — the jaguars, the foxes, the wolves, the monkey, the python, and two of the three ostriches? — Had they disappeared in the narrow alleys between concrete houses? In the rubble of the demolition?

Houses had been demolished also. Forty Palestinians dead.

Why do I think of the animals? Maybe because I remember the slaughtered buffalo in America. Maybe it is a disguise to cover the deaths of the people.

Watch out little ostriches — the ones who survived — you were caged in the heart of a warring world. So what if you die of bulldozer fright or the fright of the soldiers shooting in the streets? The destruction of your zoo was preferable to running over explosive charges in the road. You have no weapons. You are easy.

What would it be like to be caged as the bulldozers pushed through the zoo?

Who cares about feathers and long legs? Who cares about the terror of the animals? Maybe death wiped away their horror as bulldozers cracked the long leg bone of an ostrich and turned over its body as a feathered accordion that squealed an improvisational war dance.

Ou'Wash in his bulldozer. Barbarians. All of us. In this house of war.

The morning I leave Tel Aviv, I lift my luggage to the bin, that roost above the seats. My little wheeled bag likes its high places with others tunneled in darkness. It likes the act of leaving.

Tel Aviv to Frankfurt to Minneapolis. Nearly twenty hours.

Insurgents. Militants. Returning thoughts of Fallujah. An underestimation of Ou'Wash.

My family has been in wars. Woods Lewis, my paternal

Cherokee great-grandfather, was in the Union Army. My maternal great-grandfather, James Perry Adams, was in the Confederate Army. I have the small pitcher he brought my great-grandmother, Martha Adaline Adams, when he returned in 1865. Then my uncle in World War II, my cousin in Vietnam, my son in Desert Storm—

What is different about bulldozers in Gaza and car-bomb drivers? What about those men in Baghdad shooting guns into the air in a crowd? What about them jumping up and down in the streets in an Islamic polka at the death of a Palestinian leader who was not for peace. The Iraqi waltz. The Jews and Palestinians mopping up the dance floor. Their purpose. Their march. Their Crusades.

All countries have a disguise—wearing *peace to the world* while trampling into another country, in our case, to establish the disguise of democracy. Our paper doll clothing.

I dress my paper dolls in purdah, chador. I cover them from the news.

I made my paper doll dresses of newspaper. They wore words. They wore the print of stories I didn't want to hear. I gave the words instead to them.

The Paper Doll Witch Trial

Once I cut out a paper doll. I named her Job. I drew boils on her. I burned her at the stake.
    I taught her to see the spirit land of buffalo.
    Of Indian history.
    Of Indian land.
    Of land that was Indian.
    Words that were land. Land that was words.
    Everything is a trial to me. Forgive my love of Job.
As I travel with a fish tank on my back. Fold-tabs over my shoulders.
    Excuse the paper dolls on my back.
    I wash my paper dolls with butter.
    I make bulletproof vests for my paper dolls.
    Give me space. Give me a chance to breathe a moment.

Terrorists

The terrorists attacked the seats of finance and government. They should attack the churches. Within four blocks of the college where I teach, there are the Immanuel Lutheran Church, St. Paul's Church on the Hill Episcopal, Church of the Immaculate Heart of Mary, Twin Cities Friends Meeting, Macalester Presbyterian Church, Fairmount Avenue United Methodist Church, Mt. Zion Temple, the nondenominational church I have attended for most of my years in St. Paul, Bethel Christian Fellowship. The St. Paul Alliance of Churches also sits on the edge of our campus. There are churches all over the city. Open the phone book. There are churches all over this country. Maybe you have to be in them to see them. Maybe you have to know church attendance all your life with participation in small Bible study groups and prayer groups to know the standing power of Christianity. Terrorists attacked the seat of government and finance without realizing the power at the core of our country. Faith is the flyover zone. Christianity may be broken into interpretations. It may be as open to interpretation as the constitution. As broken as native tribes. But its presence is manifold.

As a mixed-blood Native American, I am aware of the anger of many over the loss of language and culture in boarding schools, and the many other hurtful ways of Christianity. I can say I speak only for myself, though Christianity is the major religion of Native Americans.

I was not surprised to hear so many mention the moral component that influenced their voting in past elections. What that means is hard to define. Christianity is not exactly doing certain things and not doing others. It is a mindset, a way of life, a trust, a matter of faith, an understanding that many can dismiss and do. It is recognition of the principles behind the faith of whatever faulty representation we make of it. It is Christ's death on the cross for the propitiation of our sins and the renewing power of Christ in our lives. It is possibility. It is elasticity. It may be quantum physics. It means, I am no longer bound.

When the Baptists converted the Cherokee, they studied their culture first. They knew there was a story of the origin of corn, the staple of the sedentary tribe. When a woman was slain, corn grew from her blood spilled on the ground. The missionaries told the Cherokee, just as their life (corn) came from blood, another life, a spiritual life, came through the blood of Jesus Christ.

The religious groups that evangelized the northern tribes were ignorant of the belief systems of those tribes. Their process of assimilation was harsher — brutal, probably, is a word that could be used. They taught Indian students shame over their names and customs. They forbade the speaking of native languages. Their method was punitive and disruptive.

Does Christianity make sense? It is anything that logic can believe?

Shape shifting. Transformation. A tricky quality of vision. Blacked-out boundaries. Shifting subject matter. Yet returning none the same. The irreconcilable differences with which I have to coexist. Or the coexistence I build with the irreconcilable differences. The fragments of Christianity in its denominations and subdenominations and no denominations. The rage at its rampage on the Indians. Why am I a Christian? How can I be?

How many times has everything been rubble? How many times have I been in circumstances larger than I could handle? I did not have the power to endure them. But with Christianity, transformation comes.

Ou'Wash sheds his teeth or faith blunts them with a file.

Ou'Wash

Not in the dictionary. No, he's covert. He is everywhere. He is Evil. E-ville. EVL. The DE-VILLE. The heavy foot in the dichotomy of good/evil. Sometimes he wears the costume of a lamb. He stirs up war. He flies a kite. Rides with insurgents. Gathers scalps on a battlefield. He has a boneyard all his own. He has a tight grip, cutting off blood to the fingers. He is a cloud coming over the earth. He rides a camel. A jet. The military vehicles and car bombs are his. Ou'Wash lays traps. He burns wholly. Promotes murder, public beheadings, regimes of terror. He counts his numbers. He sends Delusion. Behemoth by land. Leviathan by sea. He pushes buttons. He is Dictator. He squeezed shut the hearts of Indian children in boarding schools. He is a house with the life sucked out of it. He is a crippling rage. No one means anything to Ou'Wash. He sucks dry. He cuts out paper doll clothes of camouflage uniforms. The lions run from him. The ravens gather. He is a wild goat. A landing in Roswell. He wears the costume of a doughboy on a table. Dead, computer-screen eyes are his. He is a peacock. The great Dragon cast out of Revelation 12:9. That old serpent called the Devil, Beelzebub, and Satan. Horned and pitchforked. He fell in his spaceship to the earth and his angels rode with him — Isaiah 14:12. He slumps around nations to find those he can Deceive. Destroy. He moves into our heads. He resides in our will. The Dominion of war fields is his.

This Journey of Paper Dolls:
this escape from entrapment

Richard Henry Pratt, officer in the Tenth Cavalry, established the first Indian boarding school in Carlisle, Pennsylvania. He had been stationed at Fort Sill in southwestern Oklahoma, where he met Kiowas, Cheyennes, and Arapahos on the Red River reservations. He tried to work with the "hostiles" but couldn't, and he finally shipped them by train to Florida. They arrived in prisoners' shackles. They wore military uniforms. Their hair was cut. They walked to military drills.

Pratt met with Indian reformers who wanted to *civilize* the Indians. He wanted to help them adjust and enter society. His method would be *immersion*, a term he borrowed from the Baptists, holding them down in the civilization process until they were "thoroughly soaked." He would train them for jobs as servants in homes and menial laborers in the workforce. But Pratt realized he had to start the civilization process earlier. Few of the older Indians could be reformed. Pratt proposed the removal of Indian children from their families. The children would be sent across the country to a boarding school. Pratt had decided on the Carlisle Barracks, a former cavalry post that had been closed. In September 1879, he approached Spotted Tail's reservation in South Dakota, and then American Horse, Young-Man-Afraid-of-His-Horses, and Red Cloud at the Pine Ridge Agency. They were reluctant to consider sending their children away. But

Pratt argued that they would have done better if had they been able to read the treaties. Perhaps the interpreters didn't convey the exact meaning. They might still have their land if they could read. Luther Standing Bear was one of the children who traveled in the "moving house." October 6, 1879, the train arrived at the Carlisle Indian Industrial School in the middle of the night. "There was no fire in the stove," he wrote in *My People, the Sioux*. There was no food, no beds, bedding, nothing. After traveling for several days from the Dakotas, "we went to sleep on the hard floor, and it was cold."

Among other supplies, eventually, they would need a cemetery.

"Of the 73 Shoshone and Arapahoe students sent to the Carlisle, Genoa, or Santee boarding schools between 1881 and 1894, only 26 survived the experience," Brenda Child writes in *Boarding School Seasons*. She also lists the Indian children who were buried in the cemetery at Haskell Indian Institute in Lawrence, Kansas, from 1885 to 1902. Not all the children who died at the schools were buried in the cemeteries. Many were sent home. Other schools in Child's book are Flandreau in South Dakota and the Pipestone Boarding School in Pipestone, Minnesota. Tsianina Lomawaima wrote about the Chilocco Indian School in Oklahoma in her book *They Called it Prairie Light*. Theresa Milk lists names on grave markers in her book *Haskell Institute: 19th Century Stories of Sacrifice and Survival & Haskell Cemetery Walking Tour*. There rarely was adequate food, clothing, and medical care in the boarding schools. The Indian children suffered homesickness or loss of spirit. They suffered from overwork. They suffered tuberculosis, trachoma, pneumonia, and other diseases in the government boarding schools.

Though necessities were not at Carlisle when the children arrived, what had arrived was a church organ. This new cavalry: Christianity. This mother of boarding schools. This Boarding School itself.

Re: The Native American Boarding School Policy

Establish the boarding school. Do not nurture. Isolate—though there were many students at the boarding school. *Student* isn't the right word. There's a participatory sense to it—which was missing at the boarding school. If it were volunteer, the boarding school would have been vacant. No one would have chosen to lose language, family, structure, meaning, everything. It was a factory for unfit Indian children—who did not know their customs, their language, who were made forever strangers to themselves. The boys in shop. The girls, domestic service.

What nationality are you? They asked in school. *Indian*, my father said when I asked. What paper doll book did I belong in? What erasure? What removal from others?

The Return from Carlisle

> And, wrote Lee
> Rust Brown, "The transparency
>   can see
>   through
>   the object to
> a whole of which the thing
>   is a fragment,"
> as Carlyle was shown the railway cars:
> rolling stock: flatbeds, passengers, cabooses —
> | Caroline Knox, *He Paves the Road with Iron Bars*

After a trip to the Carlisle Indian Industrial School, I drove nine hundred miles in seventeen hours from Carlisle, Pennsylvania, to Kansas City, Missouri. A round moon ran through the clouds — hunting as I traveled. I had not been able to sleep but was pulled through the night. I wanted to get back. My foot on the gas pedal that would not let up.

    In the dark, the transport trucks were migrating herds — Interstate 70 west through the Pennsylvania mountains, through tunnels, upgrades, downgrades. Sometimes they came two abreast from the other way like lead animals. They roared through the night. Trucks are nocturnal, though they travel also in the day. Sometimes when I am sitting at my desk, I remember them on the road.

THE RETURN FROM CARLISLE

The clouds that night were a string of paper dolls. I was a ship passing through the straits. The bright moon Cyclops could drown me any moment, his one hand petting his beloved sheep, his other hand pushing me down.

It was there on the road, I saw two young deer, still spotted, trying to cross.

Then the moon was gone, under clouds, and the highway was wet with the smell of rain just passed.

Driving is a form of cutting out paper dolls — maybe because, fifty years ago, I used to get a new book for the trips we took. The darkness that night was a paper dress through mountainous repetitions that finally eased into Ohio and the prairie ahead. The last time I looked at the moon, it looked like the top of a pencil eraser.

Inside the Indiana border, at dawn, I pulled off the road and slept twenty minutes to let the dreams pass. Then drove on. And drove again. After twelve hours, I still had a hundred miles to St. Louis and just over three more hours to Kansas City.

Alone on the road, I visit places I've been before. Different states of mind. Despair. Loneliness. Helplessness. If anything would happen, and it has. Twice I have had flat tires on long road trips. Twice a man stopped and changed the tire. I know I am alone. In danger. There is a spirit that comes with travel. I step into it. The journey is larger than I am, but I grow into it as I travel. It is a spirit already on the land. I step into it. Surely America is a land of passing cars. There is a constancy of truth on the road, snorting, grunting, grazing on gasoline.

I long for the road. I hunger for travel. The shoulder of the road is a selvedge that will not unravel. It is a place that will not be undone. The process of travel is the selvedge of my life. Though the cloth of my life has been cut up, the edge of the road holds. I feel pushed along, fueled by the history of travel over roads. The moving cars, transport trucks, carriers. The sound of the road is a steady hum.

I remember the deer—their world intersected by roads they don't know how to cross with traffic—How to step out onto the road and not get hit—How to gauge the oncoming—What are these strange animals that pass, that kill but leave the carcasses, not even eating—to send a child to the world, to get through it all. Our journey here is to step into this. What means of death is coming down the road? Aware of traffic but not able to judge the speed, the reason it is there. What is that pavement doing there where the deer want to go?

Another animal at dawn, a small one on its hind legs, muskrat? woodchuck? wanting to cross. Its front paws held up as though in prayer.

The moon wore the warrior-stripes of clouds the night I returned from the research trip to Carlisle Industrial Indian School, driving in a night what took a week on the train for students coming to the school in the nineteenth century.

I also saw a turtle trying to cross the road. Should I stop and take it back to the side of the road? Wouldn't it just start out again?

Forgive this ship I drive on the interstate.

The need to get it right here on the bottom of the sky.

Boarding School Physics

> ...early printed doll clothes...did not include tabs...Instead children...attached the clothes with tiny drops of sealing wax. | Roma M. Welsh, *Early History of Paper Dolls*

Our tribes were together until the big bang blew us apart. Afterward we transmuted in a colder climate, no longer what we were. An atom is a particle with electrons revolving as swallows at evening. Quarks joined in with the ducks flapping their way above the highway. Their strings of webbing forces. Mass and charge. A multiple unification theory. Their big smooth words we heard after our *reduction* were now small turbulent ones. Sometimes I looked into the air and could see the mass of strings moving. After travel, I could see dark sparkles in the cold air. It is what we make of dimensions. Ours and yours. There are multiple realities. Subtractions on the blackboard of the boarding school indicated this. Broken treaties. Landscapes cut in half. General relativity and quantum mechanics on a disc. It is the sameness of the difference in the big and little worlds. They jump to different tunes while playing the same music. Our small world has gone through reduction. It has been boiled to its invisible essence. Lapping with intensity. We learned the smooth orderly world of general relativity placed on the quantum mechanics of our turbulent one. The overlay of it all. A herd of buffalo once there was not there. Our arrows disappeared into the ice hole of the target. We multiplied the four forces. We found corkscrews we didn't know how to name. The power of the new world. The old land circle. That's why strings are round. Or nearly so, bumped into their line. There are contradictory possibilities. And fluctuations on the highway. In this frenetic world there are particles of vibrating twine. The theories of two worlds not compatible, but they take the same denominator — their essence is the same. Our big world compressed beyond endurance — our ultimate theory in which we are stuck to the sealing wax of their world.

Piecework

> The universe we see around us
> corresponds to just one set of decoherent histories. | Seth Lloyd,
> *Programming the Universe*

There are wormholes in the text of memory—
    The fabric ripped in the process of inflation.
    There are empty spaces in the standard model—
    A piecework format.
    Do I need the whole when the pieces reflect the lived experience between the relationship of process and the parts that hold the physics of identity?
    I made a turtle with a paper fold-tab shell.
    He wears a costume of his house.
    I told him not to go out of the yard. I told him not to cross the road. He is too slow—too slow. He leaves with his house trailer on his back.
    I carried my house of words on my back. I have been run over on the road. I have gotten up.

These (Indian) people who were, and are now on the remnant table in the cloth-goods store on a road Ou'Wash bulldozed. American history, yes, this invasion, this making war on others, began on our own land.

In the night, I think of the Indian children crated for boarding schools.

These small sorrows we box for moving.

That constant motion, change, and woundings of the universe.

Put your ear to the earth—you can hear the voice of blood crying out from the ground all the way back to Able—Genesis 4:10.

Geographies of a Realigned Language

> By reason of the multitude of oppressions,
> they make the oppressed to cry. | Job 35:9

What is it I do speaking from the margins? Writing in the area of my academic scholarship—Native American literature and creative theory. More than anyone, I have been influenced by Gerald Vizenor. The trapezoids of space he builds in his words. He pursues the invented Indian in his writing. He disrobes the inventions of disguise. He uninvents the invented. It was the world that invented the Indian. Columbus had been on his way to India when he came across this continent's natives. In the earlier stereotype, all Indians were Plains Indians with buffalo, teepees, and feather bonnets. But for the Cherokees, corn was a staple. The men wore tunics and turbans. The Cherokees had an early written language and an ability to assimilate. To shape language to shape.

I am an invention of that invention.

What do I do from the outskirts?

I do nothing directly for the tribe in this new stance of tribalism in which one identifies with an individual tribe and not the overall Indianness, which was Plains Indian, the migratory buffalo hunter, the teepee dweller, and not the corn-farming Cherokee.

I do not know the Cherokee language. Yet the stories of the Cherokees fill my pages.

Other tribes also infiltrate the marginality of my appropriations. I wrote about the Shoshoni in *Stone Heart*, a novel about Sacajawea. who accompanied Lewis and Clark on their 1804–6 expedition. I wrote about the various Plains Indian tribes for the late-nineteenth-century Ghost Dance in *The Dance Partner*. I wrote about Kateri Tekakwitha, a Mohawk, in *The Reason for Crows*. The crows, of course, are the Jesuits who came from France to convert the Indians. I wrote the first-person narration of a priest crossing the Atlantic and the terrible seasickness he suffered.

The past is given in a knot of unknowns. I am hitched to a wagon pulling this baggage of Indian history. Not directly connected with, except for the tongue and wheel. Giving voice to those who did not have a chance to speak their side of the story gives me chance to speak also — to know, to restore through language.

Woods Lewis, my Cherokee great-grandfather, was born in 1843 near Sallisaw, Oklahoma. The courthouse later burned, and records are gone. I know he was in trouble and fled Indian territory. After the Civil War, he settled in Viola, Arkansas, and is buried in Wake Cemetery above Norfolk Lake. One of his children, Orvezene Lewis, my grandmother, later married Dr. William Jasper Hall. Recently, I had an e-mail from a woman in the Lewis family who said there were old stories of a brother who got into trouble and fled, and no one ever heard from him again. She also told me they called themselves "Black Dutch," an indirect term for Cherokee.

That is what I know. That is what I am. A great-granddaughter of a renegade. Still fleeing the laws of the English language.

What I know is. What I am is this airway. This air.

All my life has been an erasure of who I was — am. A part-native heritage surrounded by Europeans, and most of them European several generations back. They too were erased from what they had been. Nonetheless, they had the dominant fork. They knifed and spooned their way through family dinners and their side of history. My native heritage was amputated. Yet the ghost ache of it was there. Withering, dying on the vine. My writing would reinstate the limb — Would re-grape the vine.

Much of my writing, up to now, has been about restoration. In a collection of my stories, *The Voice That Was in Travel*, the last story in the book is called "America's First Parade," with overtones back to the Trail of Tears. The setting of the story is Tahlequah, Oklahoma, the new Cherokee capital. I had to go back and look at the story to find the main character's name and realized that she is left unnamed. She owns Redlands Café with her former husband. Her son is getting married to Janet Gillette. The traditional Christian ceremony is shaped with Cherokee customs. "Why hadn't she seen the renewal in the Cherokee? She had that restlessness she'd seen in her father, but she couldn't blame it on him. The only thing she didn't want was to stand still. The anger at herself. The guilt. She belonged to the generations between her grandma and her children, who were finding their way back to what she and her parents had thrown away. Now it was facing her in its loveliness."

It is in their finding that I also find. The past still inhabits the land.

"Sometimes the spirits were so thick, she couldn't walk from her house of an evening."

In the story, I also include a passage in Cherokee from an early translation of the New Testament book of John. It shows the direct translation of the word order. "John first written by him that from the beginning one that lives we have heard our eyes we used what we saw and our hands what we touched word life it happened and we saw we are speaking of that which ends not." I have used passages of the old Cherokee and its direct word-for-word translation in several of my books.

Many of the Cherokees were converted by early Baptist and Moravian missionaries.

As Maureen Konkle asks in her book *Writing Indian Nations*, how can an Indian who is a Christian and writes in English still be an Indian?

I hope that is one of the contributions to my tribe and the overstepping of my tribe to other tribes — An explanation ceremony of faith. That — and an intertribal, innovative Native American writing in which oral tradition is recreated in written form — or a facsimile or something that would bring to mind what oral tradition could have been.

I have the thought sometimes, why am I crossing these borders? But these border crossings are what my writing is about.

I'm interested in a quasi-theoretical poke at quasi theoretics. I take a quasi-critical approach to native work. A cellular application of Christianity, or at least a down-home fundamental interpretation of Christianity. How do these non sequiturs fit? These nonconformatives to one another. These right down contradictories. A blurp on native history. A blurp from Christian history. An examination of academic-faith-based-living that liberal academia dismisses, yet it has been my guide wire.

I once opened *The Writer's Chronicle*, October-November 2006, to an article by Elizabeth Oness, "Poets as Independent Publishers," where she quotes her husband, I assume, C. Mikal Oness: "In an oral traditional setting, oral formula and type-scene trigger different resonant meanings only because there's a physical and psychological locus that contextualizes the 'text' — the verbal production requires a 'performance arena.'"

What is he talking about? was my first question. But I kept reading.

"My aim, as a printer, is to recall that notion of performance arena by concertizing the images, binding, and verbal text to allow for a similar dynamic of meaning making as would occur in a preliterate, traditional setting."

There is something in that I like—and that I get on some level. Native oral tradition now dances also in the arena of the book, and in outward readings wherein an image or tone or sense-of-what-was lives again—or it ghosts the audience as state parks use the ghosting technique to rebuild fort sites, reestablish a sense of what was from whatever evidence is left.

I like to work in the vast space between signifier and signified. I like to work with a transposition. An illiteracy. A shifting meaning, a tilting of words, a transformage, a slippage, dippage (of one into another). A scrambled past retrieved in scrambled form.

Once I wrote a novel, *Designs of the Night Sky*, that is an explanation tale for written language. The spoken word is more important, of course, but we live in a printed world. The book is written in broken texts as if the scattered sections were stars in the night sky—or patterns of stars in the night sky. The idea for written language came from the stars—the constellations are seen as paragraphs in a story.

In the book, I combine a contemporary story of the Ronner family with old excerpts from "Emigrating to the West by Boat" (original in the National Archives Office of Indian Affairs, Washington DC, "Cherokee Emigration" C-553, Special File 249.) and "Poor Sarah, or Religion Exemplified in the Life and Death of an Indian Woman," by Elias Boudinot, a Cherokee leader born in 1802.

The dialogue in the book is in the form of drama—
Robert: (at first, he can't speak) "She died in her sleep."
Wayne: (he is broken up also) "Somehow she let go."
Raymond: "She kept the peace in the family."
Ada: "She came to the last page and her book closed."

The indirectness or re-routing of the novelistic expectations is a technique of poetry, the renegade genre. There is subversion of text. In the novel, all genres work together. It is a light working, but the novel echoes drama and poetry. I am interested in one form becoming another, or how in one form there are echoes of others.

I like the subjectification of text. Historical writing become *hysterical*. An illogic outside logic. All the missing emotion.

Shape changing is common in native thought. *Designs of the Night Sky* is a shape-changed novel. There are exact places and exact situations in the book. The Iguana Café, the setting I walked in Tahlequah, Oklahoma, taking notes, taking names. The manuscript and rare book section of the Northeastern State University library where Ada Ronner's works are there. The old texts are kept in a small cage in a corner of the library behind something that looks like chicken wire. Indian country also has dysfunctional families.

In *Primer of the Obsolete*, a poetry collection, I work with the way my grandmother thought — the way language must have appeared to her. She could not even write her name, but she was the bridge between the old Cherokee and the coming English. In the poetry book, the new world is painted over the old world, the new paint is not quite dry. *Primer of the Obsolete* is an important book to me because I used a play of language to explore the "conjoined cultures" I've experienced. On the Internet, I found that someone has mocked my work in that book. It's actually a caustic attack. I guess part of writing is being the recipient of flack.

In my travels, which are my main form of research, I rake over the land which is a repository of voices that lived upon it and are buried in it. It is where I find these voices — these bones of writing. It is where I transform the thought of language into bones of the sky. Story is something solid in the unsubstantiation of this airway where I find myself.

The message is there. The connection to the past. Acculturation is rough. The generations still cry out from the oppression of poverty, alcohol, substance abuse, neglect. The loss of what was floats through the airways into my dreams from time to time with an overwhelming sense of grief. Sometimes I feel my own self as a child in a grade school where I was the darker, the unwanted, the wounded, the ignored. And yet the skeleton — the furniture of restoration is present also. There was something solid I received. Through education, mainly. Any maybe from my parents.

I am an outsider of the outsiders, though I see Indian tribes as integral to the space of this country. It is what is growing in the field I have planted. A field that is fragmentary. Abrupt. In the overall battle plan, I make new ledger drawings, which writing is.

The Eskimo Wars

> The only way to be there and not crushed — is to unseat occurrence inside (once/at all/them) and not fight at all. | Leslie Scalapino, "Pal Mal Comic, or," from *Dahlia's Iris*

> Words assembled in another way make another meaning, and meanings assembled in another way have different effects. | Pascal, *Pensées*

Or: still in search of native theory: As usual, I start from a native perspective: the something that moved there. The peripheral vision. The indirect trail. The evidence enfolded in story. The different voices that move there. The personal mixed with the academic. The scholarship that is a cut-out book of different landscapes.

To look into the literature of another, I believe it's important to start with nothing and face the discomfort. To wander for a while. To feel awkward and not at home.

But at some point, there has to be connection that asks, what is happening here? At some point, there has to be contact that says, this is what I think it means.

I want to take a creative rather than analytical stand. I don't want to look at native literature through another's theory, though that is helpful/an identity in flux — which is a principle formulated by Goethe, or Mikhail Bahktin's work on a dialogue of forces, or a world between consciousnesses, or his pursuit of different answers to the same questions. He also said history/a dialogue about it/should take into consideration the interpretations and heteroglossia/the many voices of history.

I am a stranger to what I am. I have an identity in the process of being created—A theory that is a trampoline on which there is rise/fall/rise.

Or:

He came as an outvoter to outvote defeat. He came to speak on withdrawal of power from the colonizer. Non-self-governing territories with their vernacular and dialect no identity can form. The political founder of colonial status with political proclamations, thunderous collapses, lists, catalogues, prosaics, place-runners, place names, on and on defined by its amplitude. An island formed establishing a clump of mud on the surface of the water that dried and spread this turtle island, this America on the world. The terrible brightness of identity placed against the land uniformed against intrusion, invasion, words to march and settle themselves on another with souvenirs of the dispossessed. Verbal correlative became its own while investors take our funds for flames that remain to burn. What is the stillness here—he stops talking a moment to gather his thoughts, the former new colonist but no longer, remythologized, renamed, remapped, the territory of geographies. Locale and locale. The irreconcilable differences left in the margins told together the unit that would by sameness repopulate histories, reconstructed energies, pull away from separatist forms. And where will we eat afterward in this cold? This coldness. This political new land. This was ours and now is given against construction of national repoeticization with stories of translocation. I look at him talk but think how the joints of my bones hurt. Colonized by imperialists someone talks beyond what they are given or allowed to stay but they stay there anyway. The chair in the room upholstered, the elegy of chairs and wallpaper choices, their choirs that stray off tune, the literary works defalsified. I hear the litany of self-deception, a life there, a valiance of aftermaths, mainly subtraction and being occupier of the margin, the very name of our language, a compilation of others pierced here and there, a conglomerate of bushes, sky, clouds. Reconstructed, recused, reexcused. Transmorphed by the colony transcolonized. He wanted me to go because I was the only one with a car. The decolonized loved us they would not overboard they would be grateful we withdrew, of driven maybe.

Dichotomy

> This aim, I call Transposition; Structure, another. Everything is suspended, an arrangement of fragments with alternations and confrontations. | Stéphane Mallarmé, "Crisis of Verse," from *Divagations*

The dichotomy that pervades native work is evident in the layers of its narrative. It inhabits contradictory spheres or definitions at once. Or the spheres inhabit the writing. Native work is sedentary and peripatetic. There is a sense of place and migration, or the state of movement as place. It is definite yet *unboundaried*. Concrete and abstract. There is a duality in the root of its base, a directory for possibilities — Possibilities necessary for survival, for *survivance* — Gerald Vizenor's word for survival with meaning and prevalence — prevailence. Native work knows the *necessaryness* of alignment and imbalance. It is static/kinetic. Absent/present. Native work is erased and written in the corporality of letters. The body of language is its written form.

Language is creator as well as trickster that robs meaning. It is a conduit for the other world yet is imbedded in this one. Its variable units are the four directions of trick, disturb, interpret, realign.

Native work confronts the confrontation it has confronted. Fighting the always plains narrative with the necessary variousness of other tribes.

There is texture; a geology or geography of written language as conduit. Native writing has redistributed the distributions after conquest. It bypasses now the ear, the main receptacle of story. What remains of poetry if the voice is removed? Yet the always previous territory of sound is there. The geography of sound waves *ghost* or *spiritize* or *abstract* the soundless written text.

The brief thief of sleep after the cavalry, the covered wagons, that resulted in a native *dark ages*.

Maker—because you are forever: provide, forgive, deliver, establish us again—

Native work is tribal yet searches for individualism, unity, separation after displacement of the outbuildings of language—stories aligned to the movement of the sky. The moving alphabet of stars. On earth as it is in heaven.

Our bread is the air of the believer. The walker of oppositional worlds—anger and spiritual confrontation or upfrontness, upfrontedness, and the differentiations of subtlety.

Native work provides a *conision* of world views. Or should it be *convision*? Ours and theirs. Ours within ours. Theirs within theirs.

Native work resees the decline of culture, the loss of spoken language from what was before the invasion. After conquerors. Native work is its own conquesting—to explore, to preserve, to document the unknowing/knowing because its pattern reflects the nature of being.

The fulcrum in the crossroads.

The voice in regalia is its written language.

The telling of the other versions, all versions of events for a composite, which history always is. An elastic band pulled over all the folds. A transgraphic of the world—Bringing into perception what is known of the visible world and the other world by its hiddeness in other.

The truth of versions, the versions of truth or truths.

In Native American writing, it is the past, the ancestors, the spirits, real as if they'd never vanished. Native American literature reinvents geographics — Landscapes no longer *are* in the present sense. The boundaries elastic in this world.

There is a tribal centered aesthetic conspiring a transreservationism, an oral traditional halved on a construction site.

A creviced language caught in its crevices. Influenced by invisible distance. Native writing is a topography of oral thinking morphed into written words.

If ever there was a non-fit. An un-fit.

Straddling the outboundaries of the experience and rearrangements and realignment of letters. The outsiders and side-riders. Their voices speaking an elliptical language.

A spoken *Pocanhontas* haunts us with image over the reality of nography. Why can't *just be* is? Landed from the land that was. A *before* suspended between past and soil.

The question of perception also is raised, or the deceptiveness of perception. What do we see when we see? How far can one kick at categories and borders, tearing apart the rules of writing, and have it still be writing?

I translate the world into a shape not its own. Feeling the language that is not translatable — translating a world into a language that cannot translate it.

I clause it instead. Which is better?

Book Three
The Dream of a Broken Field

Academia and a Sudden Retirement.
A House, a Cabin, and a Summer Trip

The crows are at one another this morning. One is trying to drive another one away, while the others squawk in the trees.

On the Academic Front

I saw a road before me. I didn't have a car so I decided to walk. It was worth being passed by. It was worth the disadvantage. I broke down. I got up. I went on. Someone gave me a ride.

How do I weave hope and loss together?—

Make a structure of discourse with a long life.

Math. Physics. Theory were the cars that passed and would never give a ride.

Two colleagues at lunch discuss how it is harder to teach Jonathan Swift than Alexander Pope. They talk about the difficulties of teaching *Tristram Shandy*. And what do I have to say? I do not answer but could ask them how to jut metaphor against broken narrative in the process of establishing *route*. How to charge context for the *breeches* in the act of *laying pavement*.

I mean here *breeches* as in breech cloth or breechclout, with a meaning of covering or even shelter, yet invested with a divergent contextual meaning—a connotation of breaches or gaps—the foundation on which these words are built. There are breaches in what I experience from identity, to piecing together one's history, to knowledge in general, to what comes next in daily life itself twisting one way and another. These lovely splits in language that make understanding between cultures and even within culture difficult.

I Am Wearing the Dialogue of Another

My classes this semester are three seminars, Monday through Wednesday evenings. I drive to Kansas City on Thursday mornings and return on Monday mornings, getting into St. Paul about 3:00 or 4:00 in the afternoon to get ready for my 7:00 to 10:00 seminar that evening. I have commuted almost every weekend for a year to be with my daughter and her three small children. I also have two old aunts and a former mother-in-law to assist. It is the [*domestica*] exhibit from the Flatland Gallery I carry. Maybe all women do. I should have a cut-out ironing board hanging from my rear-view mirror.

When the college announces a new retirement program, I consider it — A four-year sabbatical at half pay. I decide to sign up. For the first time, I think of putting my house on the market. I begin the process of clearing out.

Another symposium on modern Islam has been announced at the college.

> What about modern Christianity?
> What if the Bible is true after all?
> What if our thirst is a foreshadowing of hell?
> Where is an attempt, an explanation of how anyone could be a Christian?
> Witch-hunt Christianity. Witched and witching.

I AM WEARING THE DIALOGUE OF ANOTHER

I am sitting in my office reading when I realize it is time for the lecture I do not want to attend. At a small college, there is not much invisibility. I close the book. I go. I hear how Islam is a peaceable religion. I think of deserts. I think of towers. I think of the papers I have to grade, the classes to prepare for that come boom boom boom one after another rushing down the stairs and into classes — these blessings, these students before me — and underneath it all, my own writing projects somewhere under the pile.

My house in Minnesota sold quickly.

Though I still had a year to teach, I bought a house in Kansas City just as quickly, knowing I was returning to where I was born and where my grandchildren live.

I had a colleague who was looking for someone to stay in her townhouse while she was away on leave. I decided to see if I could sell my small house by the college, and it sold in a day. Then I had to decide what to take and what to leave. I began packing my books. Dishes. My collection of rocks. I looked for a moving van, but most of them charged by weight. I found an independent mover who didn't say anything about boxes of books and rocks. He carried everything away in his truck. Leaving only my winter clothes and books for my courses for the next and last year in Minnesota.

I am at my desk in Kansas City writing notes. I am at my desk writing letters of recommendation for several former students who want to enter MFA programs. I have another letter to write for a tenure review at another college.

In the afternoon, I sit with two of my grandchildren, ages four and five. We make a zoo with building-block pens and animals in the stalls. There is an argument over dinosaurs. She wants them in the zoo. He tells her they are extinct. She doesn't care. Dinosaurs will be in the zoo. He tosses the dinosaurs across the room. She screams. He knocks down the blocks. I feel I am in a microcosm of war—I think of television reportage—the macrocosm of Afghanistan. Or Pakistan. The unwillingness to learn a new word, in this case, extinct. The unwillingness to understand an unfamiliar concept. The resulting aggression toward one another. The flags of one another turned upside down. The global disturbances and disturbing question. How do we coexist? How do we accept otherness which cannot be understood while I am sitting there ineffectual as the United Nations?

Costume

This is the first time I can remember that it did not snow in late October or early November in Minnesota. It is now Thanksgiving and still there is no snow. The wind is from the north. I drive south on I-35 toward Kansas City. Flags at the truck weigh stations in Iowa point straight ahead. Five hours later, in Missouri, I begin to see snow. It is plastered to the north side of trees like paper doll clothing with tabs over the branches. Now I pass the highway maintenance trucks pushing snow from the highway. Their pulsing lights can be seen in the gray landscape far ahead. Rain clouds moving eastward across the midsection of the country ran into the north wind blowing south. I call my daughter on my cell. She said they got five inches during the night. Why don't I pay attention to road conditions when I travel? Well, I do—I see there's snow on the highway and across the hills.

 I arrive in Kansas City, coming from the north on I-35. In the city, there has been more snow. I continue south on Highway 71 toward 75th Street. Tree limbs are broken. There are still leaves on most trees. The news will say that Bradford pear and maples are the hardest hit. Bushes also have been pulled apart by the weight. The trees stand like paper dolls with clothes of snow hanging on them. They stand splayed by the roads. Traffic lights are not working. There are electricity outages because of the fallen limbs. It was a wet, heavy snow, not dry and powdery like the winter storms in

Minnesota. The sky already has cleared. The sun is brilliant on the white landscape. When I turn west on 75th Street, snow falls from overhanging branches in long tubes that collapse on the street before me. Thuds of falling snow and ice strike the top of my car. It will be gone in a few days. Temperatures are expected to rise.

At 75th and Prospect, there used to be an amusement park until it deteriorated like the old wooden buildings of the stockyards where my father worked. It, too, was eventually razed. Now there is an industrial park, and I usually don't remember the old amusement park when I pass on my many trips between Kansas City and Minnesota, but this trip, I pick up the old sparkle of the amusement park in the bright crystalline air after the storm.

That night, as I start to fall asleep, I see the lights of snow emergency vehicles. It's hard to fall asleep after driving all day. I feel I'm still at the wheel. My dreams at first are a review of the day's events. Then the deeper going back that transposes subject matter, shuffling one category into another.

A dream is a boarding school that tells me how to see. But underneath are the fields I passed before corporate farming and corporate theory.

The sweet—The horror—The undeniable dream.

The regulators may be here for a while, but underneath, the everlasting.

The house, by the way, is in another neighborhood where I hear a church bell several times a day. The house in Kansas City needed work. A fixer-upper—New furnace. Air conditioning. Hot water heater. New garbage disposal. A roof. Gutters. Windows. Floors sanded and refinished. A new water pipe coming in from the street. New bathroom—the cabinet smelled like an old lady's face powder that had grown rancid. Nothing I could do to wash it would change the smell. A list a page long for the repairman. I have done so much work on the house in Kansas City, yet it never turns out—the mismatch is always there. In the bright morning light I look at the room before I get out of bed—the clash of beige wall and the yellowish wood floor. The wood is birch. Why had they painted it? The neighbor said she tried to remove the paint in their house, but it never looked right. I could work more on the house, yet the awkwardness of it would still be there.

It is in a row of houses built after the Korean War. A starter. But this will be an ender. I don't plan on moving again. Nothing in the house had been updated. Well, the kitchen by the people who sold it, my least favorite part of the house. A white floor that has to be washed after I walk across it. The cheap appliances. Not for themselves but for another. For the purpose of sale.

This veneer world. This disguise.

And on this trip, a $270 bill from Roger the Plumber for replacing plastic washers under the sink that were leaking. He replaced them with brass ones.

And a downstairs toilet that freezes up because they did not use sufficient insulation.

How have I lived these seventeen years in Minnesota? The cold. The cold. The snow covering the walks I have to shovel. Finally I hired it done. I was traveling all the time anyway. Or at faculty meetings. Or department meetings. Or committee meetings. Or subcommittee meetings. Or in classes. Or I was grading. Or writing reports. Or letters of recommendation. Or my addendum.

What courses have you taught? How many students enrolled in each course? Provide a list of your advisees. What have you done to improve your teaching? What have you published?—include full bibliographic citation. What is your creative work in process?—describe state of development. List your professional activities, papers presented, guest lectures, panel participation, conferences and meetings—include date, place and name of organization. Provide commentary on your professional work—honors, awards and reviews. What has been your service to the college and community including committee work? List any project completed this past year which you regard as one of the significant accomplishments of your career. Please include your curriculum vitae.

If I keep track of my activities through the year, I can finish it in a day. It comes to usually two dozen pages.

How many walks have I shoveled? How much ice have I chopped in the drive? How many puffs of breath in the cold?

How did I walk up the hill to Francis Willard grade school all those years in the cold?—wearing a thin cotton dress under my coat as girls did in those days—I remember leggings, but mostly—bare, chapped legs in all that snow. That paper doll clothing.

Those were my clothes. *annii. annii.*

I return to the townhouse after Thanksgiving, I drive through a snowstorm in northern Missouri on my way back to classes in Minnesota. The bad weather has missed Minnesota this winter and has come south. The road, I-35, is passable as a line of one-lane traffic through the limited visibility of the thick, gray air. The other lane, filled with snow, has not been plowed yet and no one passes. We are holding hands at forty miles an hour, the long line of cars and trucks ahead, the line behind. It is here I wonder how long the trip will be in this weather with an evening class ahead when I return to Minnesota: 100 miles in Missouri. 249 in Iowa. 100 in Minnesota.

I pass the brutal world of hog barns and outsourcing and interest rates. Cell phone fees and taxes and surcharges. Deceptive and misleading services that will take as much as they can and leave you with an automated answering machine.

It is the continuation of the Depression work camps. The people could only buy from the company store and were soon indebted to the store. There was no way but further debt. It is the same with credit cards and their companies, the direction toward which the world has moved. A hog barn. An incarceration. A stranglehold.

I am thankful Pierre is the capital of South Dakota.

Harrisburg is the capital of Pennsylvania, though it should be Carlisle.

I am thankful for a check and balance government, for three branches of government, for the constitution that can withstand the predatory nature of a nation and its people.

In the dreariness and helplessness of the road, I feel invisible, without ideas. I feel my failures, my shortcomings, my insignificance.

A Dress of Rain

Once I cut out a dress of rain. It changed into snow. Then a thin sheet of ice. It was a dress that looked like the sliding glass door in the townhouse where I stayed in St. Paul, with the snow stacked against the glass — the stack layered with different strata of the snows that had fallen that winter. It made me think of a fish tank —

From the townhouse, I looked at the evening traffic stopped on the road through the trees — the snarl of headlights in the early dark where I stood alone in the house with the sliding glass door.

If I unlocked the door and pushed it back, the wall of snow would stand a moment, then collapse into the house with a snarl of memory — the little breakdowns that interfere with the momentum of traffic on the snowy road by the townhouse I rent from a colleague while she is on leave. This place that is not my place. These storms — these aftermaths of storms — a car sliding off the road into the snow of the thickets and brush and trees beyond which I stand watching alone in a townhouse.

Not like fish that rise and fall — unstopped — or the past that circles and swims back and forth and back and forth across the consecutive winters.

These memories that intrude into the present. Those old accumulations of toxins that gather in the memory, swimming in the fish tank of the brain.

A House

I had a house in Minnesota and sold it.

The money I lost in the stock market has probably paved a runway on Martha's Vineyard or some island off the coast of South Carolina for an investment banker. Some of my funds, for which I had worked, disappeared. But the house gained in value. I remember my father insisting the house be paid off, so the lenders, the bankers, wouldn't get it. If I had it to do over, I would have paid off my house in Minnesota instead of giving it to my financial advisor. Not only did I lose money, but I paid him to lose it.

I should have paid more down on my house in Kansas City, and though it actually is across State Line Road in Kansas, in Shawnee Mission, it still is called Kansas City. But instead, I bought the hogan in the Ozarks.

I remember choosing the paint for the inside of the round house. Lone Star was the name of it.

I want to be at the cabin. The quiet place at the end of the cove where ducks waddle into the yard to eat and turtles swim to a log. Instead, I'm driving north on I-35 back to Minnesota.

I see the road as I try to sleep that night. Afterimages of trees lined with snow. The woods and thickets. The repetition of fields in northwestern Missouri. Then Iowa. Then Minnesota where students *climp* into these last classes when I return.

In the afternoons, toward the end of the spring semester, I begin clearing my office. Shelves across the entire wall are filled with books and stacks of papers. I begin setting out books on a table in the hall for student to pick up. I open my two file cabinets and start shredding the files of old advisees who graduated years ago. Correspondences. Personal papers. Grant applications. Notes. Ideas for papers I never finished. How does all this accumulate? It seems to me I had cleared my desk after each semester. I shred and shred until finally, I throw folders and papers in the recycle bins in the hall, filling them every day. I open desk drawers. I take down pictures from the wall. I begin loading boxes of books in the car.

How could someone with so little go so far? Why did I receive the privilege of all these years?

I clear out my belongings from the townhouse where I have stayed—boots, sweaters, my heavy coat—thinking of the weight of clothes as I carry them to the car. At least, I carry things to Kansas City each week as I make the trips, paring down to the few pieces of clothing I need to make it to the end of the semester.

I grade papers. I turn in grades. I sign what is necessary.

Then, suddenly, my retirement luncheon I share with another colleague. I receive flowers. Gifts. I receive an official rocking chair with the name and seal of the college. A student carries it to my car. I turn in my building and office keys. I get in the car. I drive away from the college, south toward I-35.

A Room

I have a room in my house in Kansas City where I write.

I removed the door so I could place a fourth bookcase where the opened door would have been. I have a desk that I bought at the Mission antique market a few blocks from my house. It is old pine that could have been part of a barn or shed door. It is crowded with papers. On the bookcases hang a Chippewa bag, because I lived in Minnesota, a Cherokee bag I bought years ago in Oklahoma where I lived at the time, a beaded turtle, and a feather fan. On the floor is an old basket that probably was used to gather fish from a river, and a *wooden Indian* made from an old wood pipe from a church organ. On the bookcases are a piece of driftwood that looks like a fish I found years ago at the Lake of the Ozarks, and various other mementos, souvenirs, and artifacts, including a cross my son welded together from railroad spikes.

    I write in the studio in my house. But my studio is the road.
    It is how I stay ahead of the past.
    Just keep moving, my brother said.

A Cabin

> Infinite movement, the point which fills all space, the mass at rest; infinity without quantity, indivisible and infinite. | Pascal, *Pensées*

I have a cabin near my brother on the Lake of the Ozarks in Missouri, two and one-half hours from my house in Kansas — a round cabin, a hogan, a yurt, six hundred square feet. It's in a row of cabins that line the lakeshore. I think of it with the hope of getting there once in a while — the grin of the cove, the clatter of the water, jet-ski started. A round house and a dock on the lake shared by other docks jutting into the dead-end cove. The small hogan with a loft for beds.

There are houses and cabins directly across the water. I can see into their windows, and if I want, I can hear their words from porches and yards, their conversations or parts of them like stabs from years ago — I also hear the quack of ducks from the shore at the end of the cove. A road follows the hill across the cove. At night, once in a while, I see the car lights climbing from a car that passes there.

We are together here who want separation.

In the mornings, the fog roams spiritlike on the early lake.

The docks seem to move, yet they are secured to the trees on shore. It is the waves moving on the water that gives movement to the docks, making them look like they travel sideways in the waves.

My grandchildren drew pictures for me: "Round House and Dock" by Elizabeth and "Ducks" by Charlie. I post them on the fridge at the hogan. They are a manger of folk art figures. They are the movement of theoretical strings. Children's art is a line cast from a rod. A form of fly fishing. The flight of sound waves. The walk of spiders.

What will I do without the snow? But Missouri and the Ozarks do have snow, mostly frozen rain a few times during the winter.

On another trip from Kansas City, I drive through fog that rises from these words.

Intaglio

> The *indian* is poselocked in portraiture, intaglio, photogravure, captivity narratives, and other interimage simulation. | Gerald Vizenor, *Fugitive Poses*

> Here the mosquito will continue to be called, "Devil's fingernail," and the dragonfly, "Devil's little horse," the stars, "fires of the moon," and dusk, "the mouth of the night." | Eduardo Galeano, *Faces and Masks*

One summer, I drove from Kansas City to a conference in Middlebury, Vermont. I also was writing *The Reason for Crows*, about Kateri Tekakwitha, a seventeenth-century Mohawk who survived a smallpox epidemic and later was converted to Christianity. She as born near Auriesville, New York, on the Mohawk River. She died twenty-four years later in Kahnawake, a native Christian village the Jesuits established on the St. Lawrence near Montreal. When I write, I travel to the place where the character lived. The land carries voices. The land is a workspace, a passageway, an echo of events. I like to give voice to historical characters who have not had a chance to speak — Sacajawea — those who walked the Cherokee Trail of Tears — the Ghost Dancers in northwestern Nevada. I find their voices on the land, or rather, maybe in the passage across the land.

Ten years earlier, for my novel *Pushing the Bear*, I drove the nine hundred miles of the removal trail the Cherokee followed — from

Georgia and North Carolina through Tennessee, Kentucky, a corner of Ohio, a corner of Illinois, the width of Missouri, a corner of Arkansas to Fort Gibson, Indian Territory, picking up voices that waited along the way. I remember sitting in my car on the east bank of the Mississippi River in the summer heat when the river was at flood stage, listening to the voices that crossed the ice-infested river during a frigid winter nearly 150 years ago. Nearby was a cemetery with a small plaque stating that Cherokees had camped there on their journey west. There had been between eleven thousand and seventeen thousand. Historical records don't always agree.

The Middlebury trip in the rain was 3,160 miles. I was home in Kansas City a week before I left for a workshop at the Autry National Center in Los Angeles, with a stop in Texas on the return, for a 4,347-mile trip. My studio is in the process of migration. As I say in my essay "Transmotion," in *In-between Places*, "My sense of place is in the moving." It is not stationary, but a relationship between places and the purpose of being there. My sense of place is where language becomes aligned to the fundamental *campfire of being* in a place. A recognition of the accumulation of voices there. An evidence. It is the invention of the first spark all over again.

I work with a pencil and pad of paper during the day—my laptop in the motel in the evening. My studio also is within the language I pick up from *place*. I find direction from this *sense* I receive—from being in the *place* where voices are *heard*.

> It must be at this time that they would say,
> now things in the ground are coming out,
> perhaps this moon,
> perhaps (when) the next will stand
> Coyote Made Everything Good. | Dell Hymes, "Now I Know Only So Far," from *Essays in Ethnopoetics*

There are old native stories of "things" coming from the earth —Animals from their burrows, certainly, and plants from their seeds, and in some tribes, man himself came out of the ground, but there are other "things" coming, which are the stories the land embodies, the mystery, the interrelationship of the layers. Writing has spatial relationship to time and place. It is in the energy field between them, creating geography of its own.

In California, it was the intaglios that came from the earth, not quite out. Driving south on California State Route 95 toward I-10 to continue to Texas on my second trip, I passed a sign for the Blythe Intaglios. I knew of the Peruvian intaglios, though I have never seen them. I remember the Turtle Mound intaglio near Little Cut Foot Sioux in northern Minnesota, but I didn't realize there were others.

I turned around, went back to the entrance, and drove into the desert basin toward the Big Maria Mountains — the intaglios looking something like the moatlike configurations of shallow gravel pits after strip mining. But they are not that — these abstract compositions — these concave symbols — possibly of Mastamho, the creator of life, and his helper-god, Hatakulya, his mountain lion, his pet, who assisted in creation.

The Blythe Intaglios in southeast California, State Route 95, are similar to the ancient drawings in the Nazcan desert of Peru — large figures engraved in the earth instead of *cameoed* — a primitive Fauve or wild-beast movement? — A forerunner of Matisse? These Indians were not builders of mounds, but with digging sticks and makeshift buckets of some sort must have hauled dirt out for the intaglios along the three-mile trail.

An information plaque said that not even the Mohave and Quechan Indians of the Colorado River Reservation know for sure what the coiled serpent and the other figures mean — these geoglyphs — the darker, top layer scraped away to expose the lighter layer of soil below, mysterious as the doodles and stick figures drawn on a scratch pad or the way dreams at night invade the desert plain of sleep. As I drove and walked between the intaglios, I felt the little tailhooks of the past. It was a history lesson in another way. A lesson in the inversion of history.

As I left, I saw a circle of rocks where a fire had been and knew the nearby Indians still used the site. I picked up a small rock outside the circle. It looked like a wooly mammoth, petrified and shrunken without legs or tusks or *shag*. I saw fossils in the rock, one of them made an eye — an intaglio itself — like the slice of a miniature kiwi fruit. The rock bore other strange markings in its squat, stocky body — Bite marks from other beasts or arrow marks from prehistoric Indians out for supper — or looking for ceremony — for hope — for something hard to find — the full patterns seen only from above.

The land carries weight. The native concept of land is hard to reconcile with the Bible's *subdue the earth*. Yet Deuteronomy 21:23 says, don't defile the land. In the Bible, I see traces of the recognition of the earth as a living being, which is central to native thought. In Genesis 4:10, God tells Cain, the voice of your brother's blood cries from the ground. I find the same cries in travel, not always blood, but events. There are resonances in the land — An alignment of one standing on the land to ones who once stood on the land. A relationship to their *presence*. I receive them on the antennas of awareness. Little chinks of electrical impulses between then and now. Little rows of invisible crops. Leftovers. Not even complete thoughts. A ratio of space in a spatial inversion — a turning of space time on its ear. Its spatial ear. Space time where events are backed into the present happenings on the land — a sketchbook of inaudible transmissions for the passing traveler who asks to see — a reversion to other layers under the earth. An awareness of the clink of hoe into the ground, digging earth to mark intaglios, to say, this is where the work was done. Language coiled into itself to make *heard* the speaking of the land. It is a realization of more moving than what is seen. These intaglios are the receptacles.

On the road, the momentum of travel pulls at places such as the Blythe Intaglios as if dragging the past uncovered, or at least a visage of it, or a flash of it transposed into a place that can't actually receive it, yet it is there nonetheless with evidences of what moved on the land in the crevices between the afterimages.

As I neared Tucson the next day, the sky turned opaque and yellow. The wind was up and something was coming. I found a room for the night and soon I could smell the sand. I could taste it. As I looked from the window, it looked like a monsoon, but a dry monsoon in which sand blew instead of rain. I watched the edge of the roof of the adjacent building lift and fall in the wind. My car was pummeled, yet remained in its place. Even the room seemed hazy with dust. Later, on the evening news, I saw the huge cloud of sand in the sky — reminiscent of the dirt clouds in the Dust Bowl in Oklahoma.

The next day, the wind was blowing in El Paso also. Sand lifted up from underpasses and washed over the car. I travel for these times on the road the earth blows away.

Rocks

I keep my collection of rocks from travel at the hogan.

I hear their voices when I write at the lake — not with my ears, of course, but with imagination.

I work in moveable, disembodied pieces that nonetheless make a unit, a whole. From the constant rain on my first trip to the east, to the sandstorms in Tucson and El Paso in the west on my way to Texas after the Los Angeles trip, I often do what seems excavation work.

The land is a repository for the events that have happened upon it. The land holds voices. The land itself is a voice. For my writing, I visit the research libraries of the soil, of river bluff, of birds in the air. I visit the library of the past we carry within us, which is accessed by intuition, or gist, or subconscious memory that waits sometimes when I wake in the morning and leaves an image before it disappears. I think there is an architectural structure of voices over the land. It seems to be what I hear anyway.

Writing is contextualized in land. The land is a field guide to language. A road to the past. What is this work I do giving imagined voices to history? Can there be a creative scholarship? Probably not. What is this then? — Dressing history in paper doll clothes —

I Pick Them Up in Travel

In his book *Mixedblood Messages*, Choctaw-Cherokee-Irish writer Louis Owens says much about the land. "Tribal people have deep bonds with the earth, with sacred places that bear the bones and stories." But my favorite passages in that book are about the "vehicular, photographic iconography" that had to do with "the past, present and present past of Indianness." Owens talks about looking into a trunk that belonged to his mother. Inside were "postcards written many years ago by my grandmother... from widely scattered places across America... coast to coast, Northeast to Southeast, sending picture postcards always saying, 'wish you were here.'... I wonder what my grandmother was doing in all those places. What force sent that woman... bouncing all over America?" Owens goes on to say, "The second thing that stands out for me... is that so many of the old black-and-white photographs in that trunk were of our family seated upon or leaning upon or standing around automobiles."

The land carries memories of what happened on it. I pick them up in travel. Sometimes when I read stories from oral tradition in the original language, the land looks different when seen from those old geographies of language. If I knew Mohave or Quechan, I would see the Blythe Intaglios as they were meant to be, maybe the way one understands the importance of the Bible once one is a Christian. But I came as one who didn't know the language of this particular land. I was left a stranger to it—

> Um qu hiita tuuwutsi'yta, itaaso? (Do you not have a tale for us, grandmother?)
>   As'a pai nu'hiitawat (Yes, well a short one)
>   hiisavawyat umumi tuutuwutsni, um... (I will tell a short tale to you, um...)
>   "oo" uma kitotani, louder ("oo," you must say louder...)
>   uma qu hingqakwa (you are not answering)
>   Taqpi tuuwutsi'ytaka qovisaningwu (It is known the storyteller is touchy)...
>   pai hak qoviste' (she may pout)
>   qa tuutuwusngwu (and not tell a story). | Dell Hymes, "Now I Know Only So Far," from *Coyote and the Birds*

Engraved on a Rock

O that my words were graven in a rock. | Job 19:24

My car has 151,047 miles when I start another trip traveling one way to get to the other. This *binge travel*. I left my college in St. Paul, Minnesota, after seventeen years and live in Kansas City now. I was going to drive from Kansas City to Shawnee, Oklahoma, to the Red Dirt Book Fest, then on to Texas to see my son and daughter-in-law. But I am called to Minnesota to the Marshall Festival. I had said I wasn't going, but changed my mind when they called again because someone had canceled.

I long for the suspension of travel. When I drive, I feel lifted from earth like a flock of birds. The magic is there. The levitation.

I drive 466 miles to Marshall on a Wednesday. I give my talk on Thursday at 1:00 p.m. At 2:11, I leave Marshall on Highway 14, in the southwest corner of the Minnesota. I take notes once again from the land: *The distance. The muted hills and fields. Maybe mound more than hill. Maybe rise more than mound. Hedgerows or windbreaks. Fields of windmills. The town of Verdi. The truth of fields. The gathering of trees. Pastures spotted with cattle. Section roads, furrows, dried cornstalks, old farmsteads, the houses vacant, the barns falling in, the smooth hills folded into one another.*

Highway 14 eventually connects with I-35 in South Dakota. As I turn left to the access road, I hear a grinding. It is not long before the *check engine* light goes on. I am not going to make it. Several miles later, I come to a sign, *Flandreau, 7 miles*. I know I have to leave the interstate. I turn down the road. It seems 17 miles to Flandreau. Or 77. I have to find a Dodge dealer because I've been told repairs are made by computer, which only the dealer has. And there, on the edge of Flandreau, out on the prairie where there is nothing, I see a Dodge dealer. I turn in. Someone is available. The mechanic drives my car one way on the road. He drives another. It is a sensor that has gone bad. They have one in stock in Flandreau, though my car is six years old, and I am in the middle of the prairie. Nearly two hours later, I am on the road again.

I knew it would be a ten- to twelve-hour drive to Oklahoma, and it was close to 5:00 p.m. as I neared Sioux Falls, South Dakota.

On the interstate, the shadow of my car runs along a field. As the evening sun goes down, the shadow of the car looks suspended over the median because the car is lifted off the road as I drive.

By the time I reach Sioux City, Iowa, it is dark.

During the long drive south through Nebraska and Kansas into Oklahoma, I looked up at the sky. The stars were stones in a black field. The stars seemed a paradigm of language. The constellations were shaped and named. They moved like fish swimming in a glass tank. They are stepping stones for my walk across the world. I have to stay on them or step into the mud.

I keep driving that night and arrive in Shawnee, Oklahoma, at 4:00 in the morning. My hotel room is still there. I wonder if I am off the road when I am in bed. Can I fall asleep? There, in the margin between worlds, a dog has his head on my lap. I pet him and fall asleep. He has been riding with me, and I didn't know it. I've never had a dog. Is it my old cat dead now five years come back as a dog? I don't know who/what is there. But there is recognition of someone in disguise. I just don't know who.

The next day, Friday, I am on a Native American panel. They want Indian magic, but I know the cry of a bobcat. Rustling leaves.

The voice of the wind. Someone gathered in the other room. No border between here and there. Those voices that are there. Tim Tingle, a Choctaw, also is on the panel. Several years ago, he gave me a medicine bundle to carry in my car. It is tobacco and some bark from a cedar struck by lighting, tied in a red kerchief. I tell the audience about my travel. The dog that rode with me last night. I have the medicine bundle in front of me.

The next day, Saturday, I drive to Texas and return to Kansas City on Sunday. My car now has 153,217 miles.

I always feel sadness at the end of travel. The old ones have been there. The moving ones. Those who have to depart once I reach my destination. I miss the immediacy and significance of their presence. The endurance of travel. The distillation. What is at stake. What is there. The transformation.

A Dock

In the fall, I also travel to the lake in the rain.

The yellow leaves fall on the wet road that curves down to my place on the water, hitting my windshield as if paper doll clothing in flight.

When it stops raining, and the leaves are dry, I rake them into mounds. When the wind is calm, I burn them in the shallow burn-pit near the water. It has a border of rocks, like the circle where I stopped at the Blythe Intaglio field.

Behind the hogan, I am up to my knees in leaves. I rake them in the drive. I rake and burn for a day. I even bag some of them to carry back to my house in Kansas City for the trash men to pick up.

Another night, returning after dark from my brother's house, my headlights shine on the yellow leaves still on the narrow road nearly swallowed by the woods. I drive over a floating yellow field — saffron and sunflower fields on old trips through North Dakota — or the bank of a river where ancient women laid their yellow clothes to dry.

Once in a while, the thought of the leaves falling as yellow stars from history.

All this — while far away, angry men lift their fists yelling death to America.

Each of us digging these geographies of lacunae —

Writing is a dock above the water.

I see the lake from the window, a cove on a lake actually, my cove off a larger cove like an image in two mirrors growing smaller all the time, receding in succession into infinity. It all seems to move into one another — The lake, the rippled water, the gravel shore, the hill that rises on the other side of the small cove. A past that is narrow as glass. Last summer, dodder overgrew the weeds on the shore. I should cut it so the gravel could look up into the sky. Those small stones that gather on the shore. I do not think about the window I stand at. I don't think I ever have asked it anything, though it brings in the tones of the day. My place on the lake is in winter. If the window could talk I would override its embraces. I would ask for stillness. Or if in the water, these words are my water wings. My uncle bought a cabin on the lake in the early 1950s. The Osage River had been dammed in 1931. I was not alive, though I came alive later and swam in his cove on the lake and under the dock where the fish hid. A secret window is in the roof of my cabin. I see it when I dream. There are spirits who are roofers, who tear off shingles spilling nail heads. At night, the formation of stars moves like paper dolls. These pictographs without pictographs, these words-marks No Ear drew on his Dakota winter count. These small clouds of breath I leave on the winter glass.

The Dream of a Broken Field

I think of how to govern an unruly collection of essays — a collection of broken pieces, actually. How to relay the broken with the broken.

On a trip, I listen to *The United States Constitution*, a Simon and Schuster Audiobook narrated by Walter Cronkite. I hear how it became a confluence of many parts in 1788: Preamble. Seven Articles. Twenty-seven Amendments, the first ten of which are the Bill of Rights. Then the auxiliaries: It is part Magna Carta from 1215. Part Articles of Confederation from 1771. It is part of the 1776 Virginia Declaration of Rights. It is part Federalist Papers, eighty-five essays declaring how government would work written from 1787-88, and serving as reference. And part Mayflower Confederation.

"A ringing statement, a radical political theory, a brief outline for a Republican constitution, a comprehensive list of natural and civil liberties, the Virginia Declaration of Rights was all these things. Indeed, it was a seminal and representative document of the American Revolution."

I listen to the multiplicity of groundings that ground the complexities of governing a country. I want to add, the U.S. Constitution also was taken in part from the Iroquois Confederation. I write a preamble:

Excuse these broken. These lost [missing] places. Saying this to get to that. Excuse these voices that sometimes seem to come from the past. Or from over the air from some distant place. Excuse these shortened, unfinished lines. These uneven pieces. This interrupted text. These barren places. Excuse the jarred ride over rough roads. Potholes. Unpaved sections. Water over low places. Excuse this chopping through the brush to find the way. To open the text. I'm doing this on my own. Where's my caterpillar? My road grader? My bobcat?

Ascension Convention

> Christianity is the ultimate alternate history... The Creator of the universe sends his son, who is also God himself, to Earth to be born of a virgin. The son grows up, is crucified, and rises again from the dead, somehow conquering death itself. Then he ascends to heaven, sending the Spirit—who is also God (there are three persons, but one God—perfectly clear, no?)—to dwell in and re-form all those who follow him. And the world, the broken world that we know so well from our histories and our newspaper, is changed, once and for all. | John Wilson, "Stranger in a Strange Land, Alternate History"

I followed the light. It's what anyone would do. It seems what they would do anyway. I was in the dark. There was a light. I walked toward it. What else could I do? The walls were close together. In my room, there was a narrow bed against the wall, and a narrow corridor between the bed and the other wall. Above the bed was a shelf. On the shelf, a camel and desert tent, against which I heard sand pelt during a storm. There was something of truth as though it was a road with traffic that kept coming over the hill. There were cars in the desert. I don't know how they drove on sand.

To make a difficult-to-make-narrative of a world above a world, I make a parable of sorts—when there is no other way to tell a story. A parable is for hiding truth. It also is for those who want to make their own truth with various tools of interpretation. Seeing for themselves what they want to see.

I knew an undoing of my footing. Sometimes I get over it. Other times I'm pulled into it again. But always, when looking for a straight road, I consider the overlay of contradictory interpretations on difficult material. It depends on perspective — what is inside the interpreter guiding the interpretation.

I went to church with my parents as a child. I remember the classroom at Trinity Methodist on Armour Boulevard where I spent my first decade. A thin rug over the hard floor. The little cluster of small chairs. As my father was transferred, I went to other Methodist churches across the country — all priding themselves on having no outstanding doctrine.

In Sunday school, I saw the storms at sea. I saw the flock of sheep. I saw my name on one of them, as shepherds in New Zealand and Australia mark their sheep with a glob of paint. I was confirmed in a Methodist church. I want to say, confined in the Methodist Church. I was married in a Methodist church. My children were baptized in a Methodist church. I heard my first revival in a Methodist church. I came to Christ in a Methodist church, then left because I was a zealot according to their standards.

Christ is Lord, I proclaimed at the altar. It was too much for them.

I found a church outside the Methodist church. A fundamental, Pentecostal church, wherein I found strength to walk through the fire. Or the Holy One who walked with me had strength to walk through the fire. I simply followed, as I said in the beginning.

I can't I say have seen miracles, other than the substance that became my endurance. I haven't seen miracles, other than, in the desert of my childhood, a camel arrived. Eventually, there was a shelf life in this other world where I climbed.

Overall, I saw a truth that I recognized as truth. Would I close the book and continue with my life, or would I enter it by letting it enter me?

I studied Revelation with several people. I had not gone to a Bible study, but I knew we sat at the table and studied the Bible. I had been in darkness. I saw the light. Not an imagined light, but the Real Light, which accompanied the table light.

We called our study group the Ascension Convention.

It is what a church is, not an ameliorating church. Not ecumenical. Not bringing everything together under the name of religion. But separating the sheep from the goat. The wheat from the tare. Jesus is the way, no one comes to the Father but by him—John 14:6.

We went to the convention longing for renewal. I tell you, I saw my life as darkness in the sight of God's light, which was the determining factor. I saw a light, vibrant, dazzling, converting. Then it seemed to dim. Then we gathered for Bible study. We were refreshed. We had converged. We made off with heaven's blessings.

The study was altogether an opening of the rages of the earth. As though I didn't know, being seeped in darkness. For some, it had been a while since they had seen the dark. Maybe they had forgotten. Maybe it had been washed away. For me it was more recent. Daily, in fact, until my conversion, and then, at times, I still was at war. Maybe there were shades of darkness. Maybe it was different for different ones. Not as dark as dark can be.

What is truth?—The space of truth. The place truth inhabits.

Or it may be the definitions of darkness that separate us. For me, darkness is a place without Christ.

In fact, I fought to get through life. Embattled, as I said, alone on the road with my exuberances, my failures, my sand traps.

I remember how church lived somewhere above us. The family could not quite struggle to where church was. We might have been inside the building, but we were not there. It did not leave with us, as I always thought it should, hoped it would. I learned that church could not come where I was. Or I could not go where it was. At that time, anyway.

Trauma could have prevailed, but I decided faith would be the road through it.

Christians believe America was founded on the principles of

God. Unlike Russia, South America, Africa and the rest of the world. The other great empire, Rome, was made Christian by Constantine, although much of it in the New Testament, before Constantine, is anti-Christian, i.e., the persecution of believers by the Roman government.

America is ruled by a Constitution, this piece of classic literature, an early work of nonfiction that relies on interpretation. This treatise that allows a collage of people to coexist, with struggles in the area of civil rights, economic inequities, class boundaries, and all the general storms of human life, yet somehow entails a world recognition of a place where things work and citizens have been guaranteed fundamental freedoms by the Bill of Rights. There are no mass rapings. Ethnic cleansing is under wraps. And we are free to study the Book of Revelation.

Imagine this place without the Constitution—this body of writing with four walls on a page. A bed of text in the middle, not pushed to one wall. To hold our freedom in check and balance, which it needs to be.

Imagine this place without *church*.

For some reason, our backyard was dirt. I don't know why grass didn't grow. Maybe it was a shade tree. Maybe we had worn the grass away by our playing. I remember my mother trying to ride my bicycle and being unable to. I remember the hose on the ground, a trickle running from it, the trickle raised above the dirt like a vein as it ran from the hose, as if it did not want to mix with the dust.

John was on the island called Patmos when he heard a voice. He turned to see who it was. The man's head and hair were white like wool. His eyes were a flame of fire. His feet were like polished brass, as if he stepped from a furnace. A sash was tied around his chest. When he spoke, his voice had the sound of many waters. He came like the wise men bearing gifts, which he handed out according to the way we believed and maybe behaved. To some he gave a white stone, to others, the morning star.

Now how could I link this to ordinary life? How do I attend the Ascension Convention, then get in my car and return to my house?

I also took notes. Writings from John's writings. The Bible is another piece of classic literature with four walls and little to say for itself, or explain about itself, in fact, as far as reality goes. Possibly I should say, my reality, for I have learned it is somewhat different from that of others.

There seems to be a hard truth of destruction in Revelation, or a truth of sorts for those who believe it is truth. At the Convention, we did.

My father was cut off from his family, maybe by choice. He never spoke of them as he sat across from my mother with her plate of cold cuts for supper. After he worked in the slaughterhouse all day. The components of family somewhere over us that somehow never descended upon us. We lacked a statement of beliefs that was stated in the Nicene Creed in 325 AD. We said it each Sunday, but it passed from our mouths as wind without rain.

In 1084, Christianity divided into Roman Catholicism and Eastern Orthodox. Then came the barbarian onslaughts and crusades. In 1453, the Ottoman Turks invaded Constantinople. It was under siege: cannons pounding away at the walls. The Turks dug holes under the walls to weaken them. Constantinople was vulnerable on the underside. The Muslims entered the city and that was the end of the Roman Empire.

A brooding mother, the invasion of Constantinople in our kitchen, the struggle of our family with its weakened walls, the overlay of the Nicene Creed to take into the captivity that always was with us.

Some description in higher language, as I said — A way of saying that opens a trail, a migration, a journey that going is. Some other abode was what I sought. A making of journey that happened even when I was a child. A traveling away from confinement, which life was at the point of finding a way away. Faith was the abstraction to handle the discovery of a brokenness of language to reach what couldn't have been reached if it remained in one piece.

I learned it in the Bible. The abstraction of message. The making of parable, which is the art of language.

Is not the earth a voice made visible?

After this, John heard a voice like a trumpet that said, Come, I will show you things that must happen. Inside the door, John saw a throne, and surrounding the throne, beings with four faces covered with eyes. At the convention, I became a lover of the four-faced beings with the faces of a lion, a calf, a man, and an eagle. Day and night they stood before the throne saying, Lord God Almighty, who was, and is, and is to come. And out of the throne came lightnings and thunder. And, because the man John saw when he was on Patmos wore a sash around his heart, it was a time of judgment. This was unwelcome news. The coming wave. I could feel it in the air. On the shelf, I had never heard the sand pelt the tent in such a way.

There was a woman at the Convention always asking obscure questions that sent us on a Biblical search for the answer. Meanwhile sidetracking us from our study. Each week it was something else. How to quiet her with a rag in her mouth. Our Convention hostage.

There was a book. Who was worthy to open? No one. No one. John was overcome with grief and cried. But one of the elders told him not to cry. The Lion of the Tribe of Judah, The Root of David, could open it. And John saw a Lamb as though slain who took the book and opened it—It had to be Christ. By cross-reference, and maybe some common sense, as if faith had any closet of reason in it.

The Lamb was worthy to take the book, and open the seals; for he had been slain and redeemed us to God by his blood out of every kindred, and tongue, and people and nation, and had made us to God a kingdom of priests.

ASCENSION CONVENTION

How do I visit this? How to I estimate what it means as I sit in traffic, as I lie on my bed held by four walls with the desert tent on the shelf open to storms above the bed? How do I say, the Lamb of God is holding a book. When he opens it, judgments fall on the earth.

I could tell them. I could pull them aside. But would they listen? Not today.

In Sunday school, we heard stories from the Bible. Sometimes I climbed a rope let down from the shelf above my bed. These journeys are what accompanies truth — the size out of proportion as though I could climb to a shelf above my bed, even as a child, yet the trip was there. The ascent. I have known it all my life. I bring the tidings out of darkness. My word for the week — tidings, as I had seen the ocean once and knew its tidings. But this was news of a different sort, though along the same line. Those variations of waves on the shore. Coming so far and no farther.

What am I talking about? I ask myself. Parables of faith. Faith that rises yet cannot speak directly of itself. Otherwise, it would knock the shelf off the wall.

How could I understand incorruption when I have walked with corruption? How could I understand the things with which I had grown up? How could I understand the Old One, the Most High, when I had been sidetracked off the main?

It amazes me how often the Most High remains quiet as the fish.

Constantinople was the capital of the Roman Empire from 330 to 395 AD, the capital of Byzantine Empire from 395 to 1453, and the capital of the Ottoman Empire from 1453 to 1923. It is the present-day Istanbul. America always was America. Even though the Indians had a different name for it.

The four horsemen of the apocalypse bring war and famine and disease and death. Haven't they already arrived in those nations far away on dark continents? Isn't there already a toehold?

The seven trumpets, the seven seals opening from the seventh trumpet, and seven more catastrophes opening from the seventh seal. Isn't that the way it is? — A part within a last part opening into another part. And under the altar were those slain for the word of God and the testimony they held. During that time, there again will be persecutions/beheadings of those who believe.

I thought of the Ottoman Turks when I sat on the ottoman at the foot of our sofa. My mother spoke of it often. I wondered if the Turks had given it to us.

An earthquake battered the tent on the shelf, the walls of the room, the bed underneath the shelf. The wooden camel clunked the shelf when it fell. How many times have I set it back up? Mountains and islands moved out of their places. Stars fell to earth. People hid in caves and rocks and cried out for the mountains to fall on them. What will they do in the hail and fire? What will they do when the bottomless pit is opened, and smoke rises like the smoke from a great furnace until it darkens the sun and moon?

Then war and more war. More plagues and suffering. Disruptions and intrusions and inversions and reversals and interruptions. Events of upheaval of this magnitude.

When my father was transferred to other packing houses, he burned what we didn't need any longer. In those days, we were allowed to burn in a burn-barrel in the backyard.

I continued to drive in traffic to the Convention with my belief that Christianity is the relationship between fault and vigor. Until at last I can say, we have ascended, and night and day we stand before the throne saying, Holy, Holy, Holy.

The woman with her sidetracking questions asked where the prince of the air of Persia withstood an angel who was on his way to help Daniel. We looked but couldn't find it. As we continued, I still had an eye in Daniel.

Afterward I got out my concordance and found the passage in Daniel 10:12-13 — From the day you prayed, God heard your prayers, But the prince of the kingdom of Persia withstood me twenty-one days. But the angel finally got through with his answer.

Others with Daniel didn't see the angel, but a great quaking fell upon them, and they fled to hide themselves. The Apostle Paul also saw something others didn't on the road to Damascus. At the rapture also — Christ is a voice calling for all, but it is a voice only some hear. To others, it will only be thunder on the horizon. How many things are going on we don't know?

There were times I wanted someone to come and break through, but there were times no one came, and still I knew there was a God. Was it a testing — looking like he wasn't there when he actually was. I decided Christianity was not easy. God could leave me in the wilderness if he wanted, for a while anyway, but then there would be a way out. Or had there always been angels trying to get through?

Who knows? But the point, possibly, is that messengers are sent, even if it takes a while. If I haven't seen them, I have felt them on the road pulling a collapsible camper. I saw the possibilities. And in the excitement of possibilities, the openings that did not restrict or constrict my situation.

It is in darkness I came to see Christ. It is where I made this zealot flight.

My parents are dead now, taking their distortions with them. I am left with the reshelving of traffic. I am left sorting through the mix of the ordinary horror of our lives.

Into all the darkness where I drove — out of the darkness from where I began — to that spot of light in the imagination — in the calling from above with its policy of transubstantiation. Its elastic literature moving out of darkness to find the multiplicity of light.

The doctrine of disbelief turned into belief. In all the troubles still troubling. The terrorisms, the upheavals, the moves to a new place, a new room, the shelf nailed up, the desert tent and camel there. The aggression of America. Who knows what our placement of soldiers is holding back. Other than the establishment of our democracy on oil rights.

In the backyard, the black smoke rising from the burn-barrel with the things I couldn't take with me when we moved. Toys, memorabilia, an assortment of papers and school projects, old clothing—a strapless formal with tulle skirt—my whole world based on the smoke rising from the burn-barrel. NO!—I called my things back from the fire—from their time of extinguishment. From the time when the Quiet One, the Fish, makes his mysteries known.

At the Convention, I often realized how the past moved through the words of scripture. Often I waited for Jesus to step out of the arcane. When all the mysteries of God were finished and I understood the berefts I had.

Yet on the road, in all my drivings, one evening in winter on the way to the lake, I saw a scene as if I had ascended to the shelf. There was snow through the woods, a few russet leaves still cluttering the trees, but along the horizon the heavy clouds had lifted, and there was a slice of evening sky, amber, shiny, metallic. The beauty and solidness of it nearly pulled me of the road. How often I have had these visions as if seeing the feet of one whose legs are brass.

Book Four
Geographies of Language

The Act and Question
of Creative Nonfiction

There was a baby. Its name was Water. And it died. My granddaughter told me this at the age of four. I took it as a serious comment on writing in our time. Storytelling is there from the beginning—because of the need to be whole.

A Rocky Shelf

> I am reminded of your faith that first lived
> in your grandmother, Lois, and your mother,
> Eunice, and now, I am sure, lives in you. | 2 Timothy 1:5

I'm not sure when it occurred to me. Maybe it was while traveling between St. Paul and Kansas City. Maybe it was the early retirement program at my college in Minnesota, though I was old enough to retire. I wanted to be closer to my three grandchildren. I had been commuting anyway. Some semesters, leaving after classes, it was dark before I made it to Iowa. There also was the weather, snow and ice.

I signed the retirement agreement contract, which required the exiting professor to give up tenure and enter a four-year sabbatical at half-pay, and wrote a prospectus of what I planned to accomplish during the four years. It was mostly writing projects. Nowhere was the real reason listed—to be a grandmother.

I wanted to enter that world of young grandchildren that is only there for a while—because it fit in this situation—because it was possible—before they are so engrossed in their activities they tell me to wait in the car. Soon they will be on with their lives and I imagine myself a backdrop, less important in their lives, as it should be. Already, I am the outsider; once in a while, an insider. I know the tightrope between, and the frustration of, dealing with three young children each one going their own way. I already have felt estrangement with the oldest because of his insistence on dominating his two younger siblings. I don't like the meanness they thrust on one another when they fight.

Sometimes I return to my house and sit by myself in the quiet. Sometimes I even feel a slight anger. I was a tenured professor. I could do what I wanted. What I eventually wanted was to be with my grandchildren. I gave up my beloved position of seventeen years, and tenure for which I had worked hard and worried over just a few short years earlier.

I wanted to be a part of their lives because I began to see that being a grandmother was a continuity. What I couldn't do for my children, or didn't know to do, or was too harried, or unhappily married, I could redo. Being a grandmother is a revision. A chance to rewrite. A privilege to add to what their mother is doing very well, though her husband travels for his work, and she is under the stress and pressure of young children, and as with the current lifestyle a hundred activities a day. One Saturday alone is filled with soccer games, birthday parties, a multitude of errands.

I wanted a chance to be a better grandmother than mother, in an unsatisfying marriage, impatient, hurt, longing for a way out.

I wanted to provide stories for my grandchildren. "What book did you bring me, Grandma?" They ask when I return from a trip.

It is in stories, oral and written, that I have my being. On a recent sleepover, I read six books to Libby, who had opened a seventh when I turned out the light. I want to provide stories for my grandchildren. I am a buyer of books, a filler of bookshelves.

A grandmother's storytelling is cartography. It is mapmaking. This is where we have been. This is where we can go because of words.

There are times with my four-year-old granddaughter, Libby, especially, that I feel the concept of *time space* in physics. A connection back to my grandmothers born in the 1880s. A continuum of voice, of story. A physical presence of the past that I give my granddaughter, not in words, but in essence, in connection to something larger than the two of us. It is not in words, as I said, but a sensed distillation of time in a small shape that is the moment between us.

On Fridays, sometimes, I take Libby to art lessons at the Nelson-Atkins Art Museum in Kansas City, Missouri. It is where I went as a child. It is where I took my children. Afterward, Libby and I go to Winstead's on the Plaza for fries and a milkshake. This week, when I read her the flavors, she says, "cherry." As she is drinking it, she tells me she likes cherry shakes, "but not a cherry in a circle." I want to be there to receive that kind of information from her. I want to be there when she takes a risk of a shake she may not like.

At the Nelson, Libby works with clay. "It isn't ready to bring home yet," she tells me with a sense of importance, but she gives me a collage she made. It is a piece of black paper with fragments of colored paper glued to it, and a few crayon markings on the fragments. I like her work because I am a worker in fragments. I am separated between cultures, places, languages. I have the grandchildren's drawings in my house and at my cabin. At my house, Libby chooses to add her collage to a paper-construction robot made by the boys that they taped to my dining-room wall. Actually, her collage improves the robot greatly.

While she is at her art lesson, I walk through the museum. There are several of Henry Moore's pieces at the Nelson. I identify with one in particular, *Draped Seated Woman*, because I am draped with the heavy covering of grandmother. In a note beside the sculpture, Moore wrote that he wanted to "connect the contrast in the size of the folds, here small, fine and delicate, in other places big and heavy with the form of the mountains, which are the crinkled skin of the earth." Moore's sculpture is a nearly life-sized woman cast in bronze, her face a wedge without features. Almost like the beak of a bird. But when I look at the folds in the drape covering the woman, I see the folds as waves on a lake.

I've seen the chart of genealogy of the German ancestry of my maternal grandfather. No one has looked into the English heritage of my maternal grandmother. The Cherokee heritage is lost on my father's side, before my great-grandfather, Woods Lewis. Because he is not on the Dawes Roll, I am, officially, an undocumented Cherokee. He fled Indian Territory before the Civil War because he committed an act from which he had to flee. He served in L Company, Fourth Tennessee Cavalry, during the war. I knew he joined the cavalry in Meigs County because I have seen his Civil War records in the National Archives. On a recent trip, I found Meigs County in eastern Tennessee, which had once been Cherokee territory, before Removal. He knew where to run. I count my return to Kansas City as a trip of the same nature.

I want to say that grandchildren make you selfless. It is all them. Their clothes. Their toys. Their furniture. Their happiness. But it is selfishness. They are mine. Mine. All mine. No one else can have them. They also are where I meet defeat in my importance/unimportance in their lives. I used to walk into class and students listened. I marked papers and gave out grades. "Do you know, grandchildren, what your grades would be for today?" I have wanted to ask.

Even in the early days, when I was writing at my small desk and my children were young, I felt the pull between work and children. I want also to be there for my daughter, to give her a break now and then, to help her with her load.

Now, when there is a battle of the wills, I know it is their lives that are important. Their road ahead. I step back where I could have led the class. I could march into it, but instead I follow. What I have now is a departure from history. A center that a grandmother had. Now it is auxiliary. It is beside the family. They have their own lives. I can contribute and not get in the way. I give the reins to them. It is the new definition of grandmother because I want them to be independent and responsible for themselves. That is the new direction. I have to let go. I return to my house with relief. I can sit at my word processor and write. I can read. I can go to the lake by myself. I can get lost in my own projects, which is what I want to do for the afternoon. I can plan for my next writer's workshop. I can pack for a trip. I can still drive. Sometimes I don't see them for days.

My own maternal grandmother lived on a farm. We had visits there in the 1940s when I was growing up, but I remember her as distant. Practical. Once I took a chick into the farmhouse and was petting it when she saw me, and asked what I was doing with the inference I was silly. It was a chick she later would behead with an ax for supper, when it was bigger and covered with white feathers. I remember those little Ann Boleyns of the barnyard. I have found my own beheading in giving up part of myself for my grandchildren.

From my father's Cherokee side of the family, I remember my grandmother's silence during the few visits we had with her. But her presence spoke to me more than all the words I heard from my maternal grandmother. I want to provide that presence for my grandchildren. I want to have an awareness of themselves in the world.

Often, in the past, the Indian grandmothers named the children and had a definite authoritative role. It is something I wouldn't think of doing with the independent daughter and daughter-in-law I have. It would cause trouble. Resentment. I want to be the faith carriers like Eunice and Lois in the New Testament. I feel I have information that sits at the center of the world, yet I am left with duties I have at the moment, shortening a penguin suit for my granddaughter for the current Halloween. Last year, it was white feathers I sewed back onto her chicken costume when they kept falling off. Sometimes, I also read to Libby and Charlie while their mother helps their older brother, Joseph, with his homework.

My purpose as grandmother is to cause fun to form in the daily routine, to distract from trouble, to console, to call to look up. Sometimes I am aware of the weariness children feel as they move along in school, busier all the time with homework, tutoring, and activities: soccer, basketball, baseball, gymnastics, art lessons and all the dancing lessons for Libby, the doctor and dentist appointments, Cub Scouts and piano lesson.

When I take Libby to gymnastics and dancing lessons, I stand at the glass watching her. She in turn, watches me to make sure I am watching what she can do. If I look away a moment, she is at the glass to get my attention back to her. I visit her preschool. I take her on errands. I am a prop instead of the center pole. It seems to me that is the way it should be. It is worth the price.

Recently, when Charlie was sick and unable to go to a basketball game with his family, I sat with him while he cried in the misery of his illness and in being left behind. I want to commiserate when his parents are too busy. I want to be a spark, an incentive. A light. A dusty Biblical road. Christianity runs high in the center of the country where I live anyway, the Cherokees evangelized by the Baptists. I am Lois, the grandmother, and Moore's *Draped Seated Woman*. Being a grandmother is an act of prayer against the terror of the world, a grounding of faith for this solitary road. It is the times I am overwhelmed with the noise and confusion and have to withdraw to my quiet house. I have had twenty-five years on my own. But I want to stand up and join the battle. I want to ignite. To call to journey. To tell them, see how the petals of the orange roses on your mother's table are like flames.

My grandchildren are in a new world. I have to stand back and watch, as maybe my paternal grandmother saw me and remained silent. It is the separation that holds us together. I think of the secret things that will die in my world as the world of my father's mother died with her. The other day I wanted to call the grandchildren to watch a storm, but they were watching a video when all the mystery of the natural world passed by.

I have taken Charlie to the lake with me. He is wedged between siblings and needs a larger space at times, a space for himself. I have seen him interrupted so often by older brother and younger sister, he gets frustrated and breaks out in anger when trying to say something.

At the lake, I have a Jon boat, which is a small, brown fishing boat, though I don't fish, with a battery-operated motor. We explore the end of the cove. When the water is low, there is a rocky shelf we call Charlie's Island. Usually it belongs to the ducks. We motor there, a trip of two minutes from my dock. We get out of the boat and walk the entire length of Charlie's Island, four or so yards. We throw rocks in the water. They are more like pebbles. We find a walking stick. We move rocks around with the walking stick. We talk. I listen to every word he says.

Even when Charlie's Island is underwater, we know the rocky shelf is there.

In a spirit dream, where all things are possible, I sew the fragments of pebbles into a small island. My needle penetrates the rocks. My threads hold them together.

The role of the grandmother is a rocky shelf.

Geographies of Language

Mikinak Niwitabimu
Turtle   I am sitting with him. | Kimiwun, Chippewa

My house is made of words. My roof is shingled with words. The windows are words I have written. During rain, words run from the downspout into the backyard. Birds drink there. The rooms of my house are papered with words. I am burdened with words. I am overburdened with words. Sometimes I cannot move because of the words I carry. Their weight is a ship that does not have water. After steering all day I've hardly moved from where I started. I hear words say, *walk inside us*. But I think they walk inside me. There is no border, no shore between us. Often I sleep standing up. My words are horses running in a field. They are a retrieval with papier-mâché saddlebags. I know words are inside. I carry words on my back. My road is made of words. Sometimes I paste words to myself. I carry them back and forth and back and back. The sky is words. At night, the dreams are words moving. The circling of constellations is the movement of lassoes. Words have attics and basements. You can hang curtains on words. A word will not return your change. In the beginning was the word. Without words was not anything made that was made—John 1:1, 3. *Could I have a word with you*? someone says. I invite them into my house. I spoon words onto our plates. We cut them with a knife and fork. By your words you are justified. By your words you are condemned—Matthew 12:37. Someone gathers the words we speak. Someone is a wordkeeper. In the book of words they are kept. A word is a sound that is said, is made, that carries an electrical or magnetic impulse called meaning. Imagine the stress on words. A combustion engine in the cold. Just see the steam that rises off words. I belong to a club whose members and dues are words. *I can't stay in this house because of all the words,* he says. *They pile on my bed. They take my place at the table. They sit in my chair. How long will the words of your mouth be a strong wind—Job 8:2? How long will you break me in pieces with words—Job 19:2?* I do not apologize for my burden of words. They are a history that has not been heard. Words do not die. They are passed along. They overflow the viaduct. They flood. They are kept for leftovers. Nations are made of words. Words of suffering, injustice, grief, anger, sometimes finally rage. Words are trouble. I cannot ask them to leave. There is no place for them to go. The Oldsmobile once had overdrive. Oh, that my words were written—Job 19:23. I would not have known but for words. I find myself in words. In words, there is something that I am.

Buffalo Nickel

I am writing a writing about writing—A writing about what writing is about. How to write a writing that is written. Which is to say I am writing a written writing. With disconnectives and correspondences between the unrelated. A writing is a type of hide, tanned, and sometimes writing was written on hide. A tanned hide but still a hide to write a writing upon. It is how I hear them speak in the past. In the empire of the prairie. In the empire of the buffalo, which I was not there to see. I am writing the lost voices of the prairie back onto the prairie. Whole knowledges lost. A watercolor map beyond which is the Maker's happy hunting ground which if not happy at least is there.

Sometimes I look backward through a book, which is how to look into the past that is the direction in which it lies.

The truth of the light is an elliptic rationalism. Is that not the way the mind works?

What is rational about the cruelty of history and present-day tortures and mass destructions of the masses in mass graves that are uncovered. It is not newer now than in the past. The snatches of torture I pick up in dreams. Pigs hanging on horizontal poles, their front legs tied over the pole with duct tape in the presence of their enemies. We should be crucified for our sins, and have been in the person of Christ. We are a tribe of lepers who steals the goods of others with final judgment staring us in the face, and a recall of the past. Every inch is there in line with us.

Actually, it is the human will that moves history.

Sonata

> ...write on the tables... | Deuteronomy 10:3

> ...write on the doorposts of the house, and on the gates... | Deuteronomy 11:20

> ...write on the stones... | Deuteronomy 27:8

It always seems to begin in a storm — I-35 north from Missouri. The rainstorm in Iowa. Pounding winds crosswise on the road. Two trucks overturned in the median, shoved by the strong hand of the wind. As I drove from Kansas City back to Minnesota, I listened to a book on tape read by Kenneth Branagh: The 1660–69 *Diary of Samuel Pepys*, who kept record of his life as he established himself in his career as surveyor-general in the Royal Navy, and in London society. He argued with his wife, had affairs, and witnessed the Plague and the Great Fire.

I thought about the genre, creative nonfiction. Michel de Montaigne (1553–92), who wrote his essays a hundred years before Pepys, usually is given credit. "I speak on paper as I do to the first person I meet," he wrote. Pascal called the autobiography "idiotic." The autobiography is a loose weaving together of discordant thoughts unrelated to one another, full of references to others and other digressions. But the voice of the author speaking about personal thoughts and experience is there. A few of his chapter titles: "The Best Father That Ever Was," "My Peculiar Education," "Why I Paint My Own Portrait," "My Diversions," "My Children," "My Religion," "These Troubled Times," "In Germany and Italy."

Actually, Blaise Pascal in the seventeenth century is the father of creative nonfiction. Actually, Pliny the Elder in the first century AD, who wrote down everything that passed, is the father.

Inside the Minnesota border, on my way to teach at The Loft for the month of April, there were still patches of snow along the embankments. Ice around the shore of a lake. Ice sheets across the water were broken up, but still on the lake. This road I have driven often between work in Minnesota and my family in Kansas City.

It all seems to begin in a storm. Writing as well as travel. I feel the clouds, the presence of something. I start into it. Often I write in a haphazard manner, putting down images, ideas, words. I get to the trace I know from writing so long. It is a beaten path or trail left by repeated passage. Writing is a process to find out what it is about. To find out where it is going. What it will say. How to make it say what it wants to say. Its relationship to the writer. Its destination, but more the process of the journey. Writing is involved in map making, finding *trail*. I start by making an accumulation on the page. A mess, in other words — Notes. Fragments. Clusterings. Phrases. Impressions. These writing exercises are a reconnaissance. A flyover of many territories, taking notes on ideas, images, thoughts, memories. Then the work of clearing out what doesn't belong.

The nonfiction essay has its principles: detail, clarity, expediency, energy, tension and release of that tension. The use of questions. Quotes. Allusions. References to others. This is how the nonfiction piece is formed. The presentation of necessary information. The summations. The gathering of unrelated notes and fragments. The shifts to surprise the reader. The final point or destination of the piece. In "Joyas Voladoras," a three-page story in *The Best American Essays of 2005*, the anthology I used for the mentorship, Brian Doyle begins with information about the heart of a hummingbird, then suddenly he is talking about the whale's heart, then the human heart.

"I take the first subject chance offers me," Montaigne wrote. "They are all equally fertile for my purpose: a fly will serve. I do not intend to treat them exhaustively; for I never see the whole of anything—and neither do they who promise they will show it to us. Everything has a hundred angles and facets: I take up one, perhaps to give it merely a lick, again to lift the skin a bit, and sometimes to pinch it to the bone. I give a stab, not as wide but as deep as I can; and, very often, I like to turn a thing over in an unfamiliar light."

But there has been development in the understanding of nonfiction. Montaigne certainly is more than a "lick," but he hints at what many contemporary writers of nonfiction have explained.

"Truth in a memoir is achieved not through a recital of actual events," writes Vivian Gornick in *The Situation and the Story*, but through "working to engage with the experience at hand." What that experience means, in other words.

I find that the act of discovery missing the Pepys diary, and to some extent, Montaigne's autobiography. Pepys presents without summation. He gives us details of his life without thought of meaning. Pepys seems to be for himself. He worked to engage with the experience he was using to bank against his insignificance and poverty.

I think nonfiction always has been with us. I think its spirit is in petroglyphs and cave drawings. It has been with us in native winter counts, which are pictographs drawn on buffalo hide of a significant event from each year. We are map makers, mark makers, recorders and orderers of events. We want to make traces of where we have been. Nonfiction is the act of leaving evidence. It morphs into the objective essay on any topic. It is "Creative Nonfiction" in its many forms, full of irreconcilable differences. Essay.

Memoir. Journal. Diary. Letters. Confessions. Units of narrative. Various narrations. Biography. Autobiography. Collections of lectures, articles, radio commentary, media pieces. Material for one purpose or venue *libraried* in another. A catchall genre of literary fabrication. A housing of various writings belonging nowhere else. It can be a narrative of any sort. Sometimes contemporary nonfiction takes an experimental direction, speaking in fragmented passages, speaking in bilingual passages, weaving several voices together, reaching farther into lapses and unrelated structures.

I started the class with a fifty-five-word piece called "Autumn Sonata," from *55 Fiction: The World's Shortest Stories*, compiled by Steve Moss. The piece was about the death of a drug user made significant by the *essence*, or the *sonata*, of life itself. The definition of "sonata" from *Webster's New World Dictionary* is "to sound." A sonata is a sounding, an instrumental composition, an extended composition for one or two instruments, consisting of from two to five movements related either by congruity or contrast of tempo, key, mood, or style, and sometimes, by theme. The fifty-five-word piece was about a brief life, yet the title imposed dignity upon it.

But the definition doesn't stop there. The sonata form is a pattern of musical composition typically, though not always, used for the first movement of a sonata, symphony, concerto, etc., and consisting basically of an exposition of two distinct themes, a development, and a recapitulation of both themes: the second theme is always at first started in a key different from that of the first theme but becomes transposed in the recapitulation.

This is transferable to writing the essay.

I remember reading Pepys in college, long before the term "creative nonfiction" was named. In Samuel Pepys' *Diary*, he was the subject at hand. He was a single instrument. I was the relationship that put it together. The other movement of the sonata was missing in Pepys' creative nonfiction.

When I was a child I had a toy—it was two Scotty dogs on magnets. Turn them face to face, and I could feel the magnetic pull toward one another. Turn them around, tail to tail, and the force moved them apart. That's what is needed in nonfiction, the negative magnetic field. I think rather than an instrumental composition, nonfiction is an instrumental opposition. Writing is a sustained heart beat. A tightening, a loosening.

"I do not mean creative nonfiction is simply writing about what happened to me. Rather, it is writing about oneself in relation to the subject at hand," wrote Bret Lott in "Toward a Definition of Creative Nonfiction."

After 55 *Fiction*, the class moved on to short pieces of nonfiction. I used several from anthologies of one or two pages, essays with titles such as "Sudden Nonfiction." Then we moved to *The Best American Essays of 2005*. In her introduction, editor Susan Orlean says, "Nothing is more meaningful... than our efforts to tell each other the story of ourselves."

Writing comes from experience: The house in Minneapolis where I rented a room during the mentorship had a sliding glass door to the fenced backyard. One morning, the cat wanted in. City workers had arrived in the street. There was the noise of tractor and jackhammer. The cat was frightened. It was frantic, pacing back and forth by the door, clawing at it, trying to get in. I didn't know how to open the door. Nothing I did worked. I went to the front door to call her in. But she wouldn't come around the house, of course. Men were working in the street. It was the noise of the tractor, the beep of reverse. The repeated pounding. She had to come toward what frightened her to get in the house. And she wouldn't. I knew she was safe in the backyard, but she didn't. I knew if she walked around the house she could get in, but she didn't.

Writing is a hotline to one's life. It cannot bypass where the writer doesn't want to go.

The Diary of Samuel Pepys reveals more than he intended. His pride in the amount he was worth, the people he used to gain his place in society. The women he used without realizing it. Once, he kicked a servant in anger and saw that the servant of a neighbor saw him do it. He tells of the abhorrent thought that the servant would tell his neighbor. He says that he spoke nicely to the servant to try to subvert the report.

"August, the 16th, Lord's Day. All the morning at my office ... there drawing up my report to the Duke of York as I had promised, about the faults of this office, hoping therein to have opportunity of doing myself some good."

Pepys thanked God as he progressed in wealth, using people, thinking of the people he met in terms of what they could do for him. He leaves a self-satisfied report of himself. It seems to be up to the reader to interpret his work.

In *The Situation and the Story*, Vivian Gornick reminds the writer to "lift from the raw material of life a tale that will shape experience, transform event, deliver wisdom." It is the shaping I miss in the *Diary*.

In "The Comfort Zone," another essay in *The Best American Essays of 2005*, Jonathan Franzen talks about the discomfort of growing up in his family. In "Joyas Voladoras," or "Flying Jewels," Brian Doyle moves among hearts of different creatures to the sentence, "We live alone in the house of the heart." Franzen sums up an opposite thought in his essay. The two essays seem to be in dialogue, each presenting different sides, as our writing often does: "self-centered in [our] imaginings. There's no object so Other that it can't be anthropomorphized and shanghaied into conversation with us" (as Pepys did). In other words, we are the lonely — The nothing. We also are the everything. I think Alexander Pope arrived at that summation in his "An Essay on Man." We are "the glory, jest and riddle of the world!"

The lock to the sliding glass door I couldn't find was in the corner, above the door, a pull-down lock that had been installed when the lock by the handle broke. Look up. I didn't think to do that, working only with the existing lock by the handle of the sliding door, looking also at the bottom to see if a bar or broom handle was holding the door closed, but there was not. The answer was someplace else. Just look around.

During the Loft residency, I made a trip to Washington DC. While there, I saw the Cezanne in Provence exhibit at the National Gallery. "The sun here is so terrific that objects appear silhouetted not only in white or black, but in blue, red, brown, violet." That's what I want to see in writing. The *subjectification* of the subject. The distortion or warping of the subject of the essay, deliberately and willfully devising the subject for a purpose, loosely stringing events together to achieve drama, to *sound*, in other words. Not lying, not making things up for dramatic effect, but turning over experience until the dross rises and is scraped off, until the piece of creative nonfiction is a distillation of experience told for a reason, a purpose, transforming raw experience into art through rewriting and tightening until there is that necessary *transformation*, until the little sentences, the strokes on canvas, the shadows, are blue, red, brown, violet.

When Cezanne painted the quarries and forests around Aix-en-Provence, he studied the structure of the land. The writer also has to know the shadows in the crevices, the fissures, the fragments in the cohesiveness of the essay. The unexpected turns, the intrusive outsider in the consistency of the essay. Juts and abutments. Unexpected turns. Saying one thing in terms of another. Yet smoothed with a butter knife of art.

Creative nonfiction is the exploration of personal experience. But that is the beginning of the definition. Its boundaries are still being defined. Often I am interested in personal experience mixed with historical voices, especially in the native culture, where so much has been erased. When I add imagined voices to historical characters and events — is that still nonfiction because history is nonfictional? Yet there is a fiction to the creation of voice — So, is it a fictional creative nonfiction? These are the things I think about. These are the things I go over and over.

Two years ago, during a long road trip, I stopped at Grant Lake and Walker Mountain in Nevada to write about the nineteenth-century Ghost Dance. In a later trip, I continued across South Dakota to the Wounded Knee cemetery, where the Ghost Dance ended with the Massacre at Wounded Knee in 1890. My book about the Ghost Dance continues with 117 years of Indian history, including the Hiawatha Asylum for Insane Indians, in Canton, South Dakota, 1903–33, a place mainly for trouble-causers who wouldn't agree to give up their land and way of life. Later, I added several contemporary stories about the continuing effects of the Ghost Dance. Again, it was the blurring of the genre of creative nonfiction.

I think there are worlds coexisting beside worlds, usually oblivious to one another, or seeing without realizing or questioning. As I stood on the historical site of the Hiawatha Asylum for Insane Indians, which is now a golf course, there were people passing in golf carts oblivious to me and the world I was writing.

Explication transformed by craft offers a parallax, a subject seen from different viewpoints that changes the subject. Writing is an architecture of form and function. It offers a different perspective — The weaving of images, thoughts, references. An essay should provide the fact that the lock to the door is in a different place than expected. Pepys, the opportunist, is me. That is the revelation of his *Diary*.

"The essay is a notoriously flexible and adaptable form. It possesses the freedom to move anywhere. In all directions. It acts as if 'all subjects are linked to each other' (Montaigne) by free association," wrote Phillip Lopate in *The Art of the Personal Essay*. Lopate also quotes Montaigne. Maybe Montaigne was right after all. We can speak about anything without apparent transitions or connections because all is connected.

For years, I commuted between Minnesota and Kansas City, especially after the birth of my three grandchildren. It is a seven-hour trip. Sometimes during snowstorms, traffic was down to a single lane. I think how writing is moving through a danger of sorts. What will be there? How will I get through? Writing, after all, is moving toward the noise that we're afraid of.

Is not telling the truth the same as lying?

> The more men pursue each his own truth, the more dangerously they err. Their fault is not in following an untruth, but in not following another truth. | Pascal, *Pensées*

Fabrication is a necessary part of nonfiction — filling in the missing parts or stating truth in one's perspective. Nonfiction is an oxymoron. It heads head-on into itself. It is a rearrangement of events for the effect of story. It is a distortion of truth even when one tells the truth, because in the truth of family dynamics, each member has his/her own truth because of the normal warping on one's memory with in-built, sometimes unconscious biases. I have a need to see a certain way. I carry within me a need to reorder as I make sense of my world — as I write a structure shaped by the mind. I have something off in me — the way someone circles when lost in a snowstorm, which writing is. Is nonfiction capable of following a straight line? Or does our instinct of leaning to one direction serve some purpose?

It is possible to theorize nonfiction into a state of mind instead of telling actual life-events. It is possible to sensationalize one's life, augmenting it beyond truth, instead of honing one's craft to carry the significance of a less-outrageous lifestyle.

Nonfiction is a strange companion. There's a folktale of the Uncle Remus sort — The horned cattle get together for a meeting because some of them were disappearing. The wolf (the culprit, though how a wolf could carry off cattle is not explained) wanted to hear what they were saying, so he tied two sticks to his head for horns. During the meeting, he snapped at a horsefly and lifted his hind leg to scratch his neck, which cattle do not do, but the horned cattle didn't seem to notice there was a wolf among them. Did the cattle catch on? Did they chase him away from their meeting? Did the wolf get away with information to help him carry off more cattle? Did the cattle tell a false story so the wolf would be in the wrong place? I don't remember what happened. I think that probably was it. From what perspective should I see this story? Beware of those who snap at horseflies? Be alert for disguise? The story is a definition of the quandary of nonfiction—it is a wolf trying to look like a cow. This Johnny-come-lately to the genres of fiction, poetry, drama. We should let it know we know it's a wolf that can take us in its teeth and run away with us—It is up to us to beware, yet it can stay.

Creative nonfiction is about the revisionary engineering of changing borders. The elliptical process that is not fiction or poetry or drama, but all and none of the all. A process of disruption that encodes our very lives. I think I have something down, then it changes. I am constantly spit back out to be caught in the reenactment of naming once again.

David Foster Wallace, the editor of *The Best American Essays of 2007*, talks about the "total noise" of nonfiction, "the seething static of every particular thing and experience, and one's total freedom about what to choose to attend to and represent and connect, and how, and why, etc." I think the "total noise" is more of a *white noise* that covers the crowding *infinite* by the enthralling act of putting words to our discontent. Which is something like the headphones a young man next to me wore on a recent flight, explaining that a mechanism hooked to the ear pieces presented alternative sound waves that negated the noise on the plane.

I remember as a child, my father lighting a pellet I think was called a *black snake*, and watching it writhe in a long strand across the sidewalk on July Fourth. I think I could say I was witnessing something like nonfiction, though I didn't know it at the time. A lot came from a little beginning. I remember the vitality and substance of it. The *plowing up* of it like soil on my grandfather's farm. The variables rubbing against one another, the ground turning over for new crops.

Penmanship
The Return from a Conference on Nonfiction

The Real knows only distances. | Roland Barthes, *Leaving the Movie Theater*

I-80 through the harvested fields of Iowa was full of cars and trucks. All orderly and in rows: two east, two west, like the monitored passing of students in a crowded hall between classes. There were lines everywhere. The gray highway was like a ruled tablet in grade school for elemental letters of the alphabet. There was a dusty sun in the faded sky, under which were rows of cars oncoming or going before me. It was a place cleared for moving, as if the highway had been mowed for the passage of cars and trucks through the fields that particular day. There was a holiness to it, plain and pedestrian as this travel on I-80 in early November with a few harvesters still in the fields, stirring dust, but mostly, fields mowed down to the ground. In the car alone, through layers of air, there was a sheerness of travel, the careful chirography.

The land is integral in shaping voice. Travel to place or setting is central to my writing. It is in passing over the land that I find voice and *comforture* (an overture of comfort) that we are imbedded in landscape no matter how long uprooted.

Voice resides in the land. In fact, land is the origin of voice that shaped events upon it. It was the voice of the land that called the animal migration trails that called Indian migration trails that called early explorers, land surveyors, mail routes, wagon train routes, railroad beds, and finally the American highways that pass along the old trails without knowing it. (I think that's why the steady movement of the large, eighteen-wheel trucks on the interstate reminds me of migrating herds of buffalo.) Yet that invisible voice provides the *shapings* that define the placement of the American language and history in the essence of *passage*. The land defines the spirit of momentum that has been America. I still pick it up in travel.

The Europeans who came to this continent interpreted the cause of space provided by the landscape as *Manifest Destiny*. That same voice of the presence of space was interpreted by the Native American as *It is one of us. The same as us. Or we are one with it. What happens to it, happens to us.*

Native writing is about that *interplacement* of human events into the landscape. It is the recognition of the entity, or agency, of landscape. It is about transmigration of elements between them, or the transmogrification, I want to say, of the essence of language that is a type of landscape that is reflective of its elements. The route of native writing is its *re-shapement*. It is a reminder of the relationship of language to landscape.

Over my years of travel, I hear the changing voices of the land. I find that stories have layers. I pick up the different voices of the land as though they were hitchhiking there. Storytelling is change. It is relative. It shifts according to varying circumstances. It is possible that my responsibilities with writing change as I get into another level of my life because then I am able to hear another level of the land. Changing circumstances in my life help me to see these new levels in the land. Or maybe recognizing another level in the land helps me to see another level of my life.

As I passed over the highway in Iowa, I felt the late autumn across the muted road. The reality of it, yet the read-into-it part of it. How to write on an elementary tablet while keeping the car on the road, as if an act of penmanship—to register. To record. To maneuver the straight lines through description and scrutiny.

The earth was gray as lead with traffic moving like a pencil along a ruler.

In the narrow median, a man could lie down, head toward the eastbound, feet toward the west with some room left over. There was community. A continuity moving both ways. We were not isolated in our separate cars, but together moving in a united effort. This moment that appears and vanishes to return again. This passage, this travel, which life is, and remains to the end—that shepherds a flock of cars on an interstate—It seemed a pastoral. The momentum that was gasoline in an engine that moved the herd of sheep along the lanes, following obediently, with some of the cars passing, but not crowding their direction because of destination in mind. The metal autumn—gun metal, steel gray, gray-brown. A determination. An achievement. Accomplishment.

It was slow, suspended travel over the harvested fields, though the car moved at seventy miles an hour. The lines of cornrows passed the fields in the quietness and overall suspension of travel—A suspension above time—riding also with the lines of Indian tribes and wagon trains as if pencils in the groove on a school desk.

Ahead, a grain truck traveling on a white gravel road beside the interstate in a strong, easterly wind blows the gravel dust across the highway like a fog in the river bottoms in early morning. Or it lets in some burning memory of a pile of smoldering leaves back in the days when my father burned a pile of raked leaves at the curb. Or it's chalk dust after school. Or snow blowing crosswise across the road from the field in a winter whiteout. It's a filament thin as a paper doll dress. Grant Wood painted the rolling Iowa fields. But here, everything is like something else in a series of multiple images. The blowing gravel dust is not entirely its own, but belongs to the traffic that passes along this high, gray road through the moth-brown fields.

The dream of these broken fields — is the dream of fields furrowed with plow blades for the purpose of bearing crops — broken so they could bear harvest. Not dream as in hope. But in the unnerving breaking apart of the consciousness into the primitive building blocks that dismantle all that seems rational into its reverse pattern or the underside of our conscious pattern so vast it is incomprehensible to the spoken mind.

Lord, when I pass from this earth, may I be in a car on a road such as this.

Off the Road

The words were found
and I ate them. | Jeremiah 15:16

Travel is away from me now, which I like, if I am to survive. Sometimes I have to come in off the road. I have to stay here quiet, waiting until I hear the call from a distant place, and I have to go again. Sometimes before a trip, I feel the road calling. I can't wait to get to it. It is not a voice, but a momentum. A little embodiment riding sidecar to the world of enormity.

In travel, I run into a finite wall that smashes into pellets and allows a passage. That is the dream of the broken field — Passage into an infinite sort — Travel that splits open what I know with possibility. A small following in the footsteps of the U.S. Constitution that governs something larger than it ever imaged. The idea of harvest I found in the Iowa fields.

I must have had to leave someone once — I've thought sometimes it must have been before birth. There was an exact moment broken off from that moment in driving. Then disappearing because I would crack further if I understood it fully. I always find a visage of it again while driving.

While watching a play in NYC, there was a band on stage, back in the shadows. Piano. Guitar. Bass. Cello. Viola. Music was most of the play. *Spring Awakening* on Broadway. I watched the beat of the conductor. She knew what it was to drive across the land on a long trip. She felt the music the same way I felt while driving. I was riding on the open land again, though crowded in a small theater seat with my large winter coat on my lap.

I drive because I can get there faster than I could fly from Kansas City to Dallas on a recent trip. There was a dusting of snow. It was their excuse to close down for a morning. I drive because I can get to Dallas in eight hours, and it took ten to fly.

I also drive because there is language in it.

I remember long ago, when we visited my father's family, just a few times, I heard the Cherokee language in the background. I remember the sense of mystery. Something I wanted was going on there. I wanted to work with English, my only language, until that early feeling came through. I wanted to heighten English. I wanted to break it into fragments because in the brokenness, the other language could come through, or a sense of it.

It was like the old story of the girl who became cotton grass. The moving variables of what is real or perceived as real. I wanted the old language to be a paper doll dress for English. Or maybe English could be the paper doll dress for the Cherokee. Until that paper dress of language — which this text is — Until the whole body of the broken story was transformed by the o(the)r.

I would hear another language. I couldn't speak it, or understand it, and I didn't hear it often. But I wanted to use English to provide a road on which some aspect of the old language could pass, or I wanted to find a ceremony in language that allowed some sort of filament of what was to come through. A broken field presented this possibility. That was the dream of a broken field — to let something larger than itself pass. I wanted to subvert the English language to do this. The transubstantiation of language. To borrow a religious term. Though this transference of the essence of language from one to another is not on the level of the transubstantiation of Christ through the breaking of the bread of communion in a Christian setting. I want to say again—I am talking about a smaller transference of that larger transference. But in the unruly act of writing the changing perimeters, there is a road—and a driving on a road—the actual passage for otherness—which is the dream of the broken field.

Book Five
One Who Wears Moths

Faith and Writing. A Continuance of
Research Trips and Travel for Teaching

I think Christ only allowed his wounds to be touched after the Resurrection: *Touch me not*—John 20:17. We must unite ourselves only to His sufferings. | Pascal, *Pensées*

And what a story. The first thing that drew me in was disbelief. What? Humanity sins but it's God's Son who pays the price. | Yann Martel, *Life of Pi*

Another Journey

I wake from a dream from which I begin to write another journey. My brother and I are in a van on a river road. We pass a campground, the fire pit still smoking, but no one is there. In fact, no one is in the dream, other than my brother and me. I am looking for a rock, but I find a white duck, wings outspread, caught in a thick spider web, which still looks unlikely that it could hold a duck. Fluttering by it are two sparrows. I think the duck is dead. How could a spider web hold a duck? Where is the spider? How large is it? Had it stung the duck to death?

Most of my adult life I've gone to a Pentecostal church. Church on Sunday morning, Sunday evening, Wednesday evening. On the other hand, I had a husband who traveled, who came home strung out. I wished at times he wouldn't come back. It would have been easier without him. But he kept returning until we divorced. When I was still married, I cried in church one night without stopping. At this church, we prayed at the altar as a group before the service began. I was turned inside out. All the grief and disappointment and anger spilled. For a long time, I could not speak. But later, I began to write about it, trembling, carrying a house, a turtle shell on my back.

I was a duck caught in the spider web, that old spatial state returned in disguise.

Church always has been at the head of the street, the top of the block.

Terry Eagleton, in his book *After Theory*, says that Christian fundamentalism is a textual affair with necrophilia, since the Bible is a dead text. He says that the Christian wants stability while life is roughness without a solid foundation that the Bible presents.

Well, the dead text of the Bible to Eagleton has seemed to me a living word. I have made my way through many years on its promises, its *truths*. It seems a rough ride, just as life.

But I've also had the love of writing. Of connecting with thoughts in my head and seeing them materialize on the page. Of seeing the alignment. Language functionary and inflating the spreading its boundaries. I wanted to write, *inflaming*.

On My Way from One Place to Another
On the Southern Edge of the
Sandhills of Central Nebraska

On Highway 183 in a New Car with 1,016 Miles
Several Days After I Turned in the Old Car with 198,589 Miles

Before I am ready to let it go, the car is gone. The blizzards I drove through. The miles of road I passed. The purpose, the heightened awareness of travel.

It's a piece of metal, my brother said when I cried for the old car. But the car was more than that to me. It was journey. Adventure. Purpose. It was journey writing. A migration from here to there. It was pulled off my skin like adhesive when it left. I gave it to someone who needed a car. A car with that many miles wasn't worth much.

From Kansas City, I drove in the new car to the University of Nebraska at Kearny (with gratefulness to Allison Hedge Coke), then south on Highway 183 from Nebraska through Kansas to Clinton, Oklahoma, where I'm working on another project.

It was sandy in the hills when I stopped at the Platte River. I carried it away in my shoes and on the floorboards of the car. The new car transforming the territory around it as I drove. The new car transformed by the new territory through which it passed.

The moon, fading into light, was a dusting of snow in the early sky.

I started writing: *If I had seen them, it would have been brief. No prolonged longing.* What did that mean? Where did it come from?

The cross-cultural and poetic understanding of the essay has a barn in it, and a crop. It is the culture of land, the culture of memory, of the unconscious that spots the understanding like the visage of the moon in the day sky. It is the present car going through the land, the presence of all the surrounding *otherness*, even the unrecognized, unrealized otherness surrounding. And it is the relationship of them all.

I picked up a rock as I stood beside the Platte. *Her face, the lifted edge of her skirt, appeared in stone.* The otherness was there in the physical presence of the rock and the story that surrounded it. I heard the voice of the rock from the back floorboard of the car as I drove:

I was caught in the haymow and he freed my skirt. It would have pulled me into the baler and set me on the ground wrapped in barbed wire. It was a field skirt that would not rip. He freed me.

He freed.

Her cry was a sort of crop on the field.

It was a covering of wire—a presence of the mystery of the unknown going on around me at all times, the tune the mind plays while driving.

The last town in Nebraska, Alma, was a series of storage tanks and rail cars, then a brick street, and an adjacent main street with a few rows of buildings and cars parked at an angle, nose to the curb.

Halfway through Kansas, I noticed the post-rock fences I passed.

> It is estimated that about forty thousand miles of post-rock fence around the fields can be traced—No two rock posts are the same. | Post Rock Museum brochure, Rush County Historical Society, La Crosse, Kansas

From the western border of Washington County, southwest for almost two hundred miles, there is forty thousand miles of fence around fields.

At one time, holes were drilled into the limestone strata about eight inches apart. It is said that water was sometimes poured in the holes in the winter and the expansion of the water would split the stone.

It was water, then, I heard from the rock in the backseat.

It was the force pushing the journey apart.

Water in the hole drilled in stone would drive apart the stone when the water froze. It was *her* voice that came between them so their parts of difference would be known.

That's the way it was then.

A car on the road transforms the air it passes through. Its tires turning cartwheel after cartwheel as it passes in the store windows of small towns. Alma or Schoenchen or Liebenthal or any of those places named after the soul, or the man who established his name on the land.

Harry Truman called his daily walk a *constitutional*. It is my driving that I call *constitutional*.

Driving is an act of memory. Other voices appear in travel and cause other things to happen. That is what travel is for. The connectives. The conjunctives. At times, those names I came from seem to trail behind the car. The land carries their memories. When I walk on the lake road, I remember who I talked to on my cell the last time I walked there. I remember different thoughts. I don't remember unless I am on the road. When I am driving, I remember not only my own history, but what happened on the land threads through it, weaving my particular mode of travel with other modes that have passed. This is the underworking of travel that underpins my understanding of travel.

In the end, it was a trip of 1,308 miles in this contained world — in this new fish tank car.

Because

What I have written, I have written. | John 19:22

Because I have driven a dark road, and he, behind me, should have been leading as we came back at night, the children with me — I learned to drive into the dark. I thank him for that lesson — hiding behind me. I could follow my own headlights on a winding, narrow road late at night, tired with the going on alone. The unsure road ahead. The home where I was headed was not the home I was driving to, but going beyond it became home. Because I have known obscurity on a dark road where I particularly did not want to be, because I had no one to follow, no one to go with, but a sure beam, a high faith in responsibility, and the sense a destination would be there when I reached it. I also had the idea of faith. Not Hegel, Kant, Schopenhauer, but Moses, Isaiah, John on Patmos, David, Job, Esther. I do not know why we were in two cars. Maybe I had gone earlier and he had driven there after work. It was his mother's house, fifty miles north, we were returning from. A place I did not like to go. I learned to live without connections, except for the going toward.

Re-entry

What exactly does faith mean? As in "religious faith," "faith in God," etc. Isn't it crazy to believe in something that there's no proof of? | David Foster Wallace, "Joseph Frank's Dostoevsky," from *Consider the Lobster*

Without a complex knowledge of one's place, and without the faithfulness to one's place on which such knowledge depends, it is inevitable that the place will be used carelessly, and eventually destroyed. | Wendell Berry, "The Regional Motive," from *A Continuous Harmony*

You live enslaved in the piece's language, its diction, its universe of imagery, and there is no way out except through the last sentence. | E. L. Doctorow, *Creationists*

In January 2008, I drove 720 miles to Gambier, Ohio, to teach at Kenyon College for the first of two winter semesters. It's a remote area, fifty miles northeast of Columbus.

I live in a large, old, three-story, white frame house on the edge of a woods. I have seen a skunk lumbering across the yard when I sit at my desk. The deer stand outside my window. The house has large-paned windows. It seems sometimes all windows and doors that open nowhere and everywhere. I will not be afraid when I lie in bed at night.

What will I do when the forest calls my name? What if I look at the sun when it shines, or the moon walking in brightness? —Job 31:26—What if my mouth kisses my own hand? —Job 31:27—What am I before you, Lord, that you would have mercy?

And they heard the voice of the Lord God walking in the garden in the cool of the day— Genesis 3:8. —What is the voice of the Lord God walking? Does a voice have legs? Are there feet in a voice? Toes? They heard the voice of the Lord God walking—Maybe it means they were walking when they heard the Lord's voice. But that is not what the scripture says. It was the walking voice of Lord God/the voice of the Lord God walking they heard. Adam and his wife heard it. And they knew they were separate from that voice they heard walking. The NRSV says, They heard the sound of the Lord God walking in the garden in the evening breeze. The Message says, They heard the sound of God strolling in the garden—But I return to the King James. It was the voice of the Lord God they heard walking.

In the house sometimes it seems like someone is walking. There is a sudden crack somewhere, then another. The floors are uneven. There is a small rock in each room holding the door open. Maybe the house is still settling. Maybe the house is walking toward the woods at night. Maybe it creaks in the cool of the cool of the night. Often the house seems more than it is.

A table has legs but does not walk. The chairs also. But the Lord God's voice does not have legs, yet it walks.

What is faith but a yard by the edge of the woods where deer come to eat?

Is the voice walking the part of the voice with meaning the ear hears and remembers? —

That becomes a physical landscape in one's thinking? The Word made flesh? —An awareness, an understanding, a spiritual engram, though there is no such term.

An engram is a permanent effect produced as a result of stimulation. It serves as the basis for memory—That is from *Webster's New World Dictionary*. Something happens that impresses or stimulates the mind and therefore it is remembered. That is an engram—the permanent impression that is retrieved later, often by association, such as a madeleine in Marcel Proust's *Remembrance of Things Past*, when the smell of pastry recalls an early experience and the present and past coexist. Many engrams form the fluid pattern of memory.

At the 2008 Associated Writing Programs Conference in New York City, I heard a friend and colleague from Minnesota, Madelon Sprengnether, talk abut Daniel Schacter's book *Searching for Memory*. It was a panel on memoir writing and the issue of memory and its sometimes unreliable nature and how to assemble the past when writing.

Schacter is a neuroscientist at Harvard.

The point of Sprengnether's talk was that Schacter's research on memory showed that the act of remembering also was one of creating. Through CT and MRI scans, Schacter observed activity in several places in the brain during the act of remembering. He concluded that when we remember we create new patterns in the process of remembering. Remembering is not only an act of recall, but one of reconstruction and even creation.

It is the reconstructing that interests me—especially in the transference of that concept to faith. Reconstruction is something I need. When I study scripture, or when I remember scripture, I am changed in the process. It is an active agency.

The present changes the past, according to Schacter, as scripture changes the present circumstances or changes the self that is going through those present circumstances. This is the operational effect of scripture on the human mind in the restructuring of old patterns. There is change, renewal, actual transformation in Christ. The Word made flesh, certainly, but also the flesh made Word, or my flesh brought into alignment with the living Word—

> As we have borne the image of the earthly, we also shall bear the image of the heavenly. | I Corinthians 15:49

I like the thought that memory is a pool or maybe a sea in which there is no hard drive of memory, but ever-changing patterns relative to one another. Our minds are not computers where memories are stored, but a living place of interactive energy between then and now.

All the time Sprengnether spoke, I kept thinking of the transformation I had experienced through faith—the spiritual engrams of faith that scripture had marked in my thinking.

I will not fear when I lie in bed at night in the large house when rain scatters on the roof and somewhere there is the sound that seems like someone is breathing. Maybe a branch fingers the roof above the attic.

Sometimes I hear a filament of rain that falls into the fireplace in the room where I work: this study that spreads to foyer, living room, dining room, kitchen, den. Above the first floor are four bedrooms. And above them, the attic.

What is this place I have entered?—This faith that is still as the house, yet creaks mysteriously with the noise of dreams and mice somewhere in the walls.

If I covered my transgression as Adam—Job 31:33—you would find me. I cannot hide myself from you. I will be alert as the deer that step into the yard with terror and gratitude. I will not be afraid when I lie in bed at night in the dark that seems to speak while moving.

Sometimes I think I feel something else moving—something

larger going on—something deeper, broader. The *squeak lines* of America are rumbling. The fabric of America I knew as a child and young adult has changed, the way old taffeta takes on a different hue. The fault lines in America's past are here. There is a wobbliness in the world. Tension on its structure. An intentional erosion in the pilings that could bring down a bridge.

Now there are branches of lightning in the sky. Now there is the sound of thunder in the house. It rattles the large-paned glass. The house itself seems to shake.

It is the voice of the Lord God walking? If my hand cried out against me, where are you, Lord? Let me be weighed in your even balance—Job 31:6. Let me remind you, I am washed in the blood of the Lamb—Revelation 12:4. I worship you as deer that come from the edge of the woods willful as prayer. I will not be afraid in this house that is not mine, but only mine to stay in for a while until I leave.

What will I do when God rises up—Job 31:14. Who is as arduous as the Lord?

At a 2008 conference, The Festival of Faith and Writing, at Calvin College, I attended a panel on Wendell Berry. I heard John Leax talk from "Memory and Hope in the World of Port William," his chapter in the book *Wendell Berry: Life and Work*. Somewhere in his talk, Leax quoted Berry's *Hannah Colter*: "When you remember the past, you are not remembering it as it was. You are remembering it as it is. It is a vision or dream, present with you in the present, alive with you in the only time you are alive."

Leax, in his essay "What Narrative Theology Forgot," from *First Things*, August/September 2003, also mentioned St. Augustine, who was concerned with memory in Book 10, chapters 8–13, of his *Confessions*. Leax quoted an article by Alan Jacobs: "Augustine in the confessions repeatedly wonders at the faculty of memory precisely because it allows us to revisit events of our lives and discern the trajectory that they describe."

Leax finished by quoting the Catholic writer Henri Nouwen, who said that "memory never copies the past, it brings the past into the potentially healing present. It breathes new life into a bygone reality and replaces it with a new context."

That is what I have in scripture — a new context for my old self.

Once again, I was reading a book for a talk I was going to give when I found the same trail. The book was Joseph Roach's *Cities of the Dead*. "The kinesthetic imagination... inhabits the realm of the virtual. Its truth is the truth of simulation... of daydreams, but its effect on human action may have material consequences... This faculty, which flourishes in the mental space where imagination and memory converge, is a way of thinking through movements — at once remembered and reinvented."

Beyond the woods on the road to Columbus, there's a place where the harvested fields rise like Indian mounds. I see them in a reinvented memory of what was once on the land, and I am called to the feet of your voice, Lord God.

The Coldest Night in Texas

January 17. I set the alarm for 4:00 a.m., but I am awake at 3:00.

Before I slept, I listened to the rain off the roof of the house in Gambier, Ohio, a house with which I am not familiar. I was afraid I would not be able to sleep, but I knew I finally slept because when I woke, it was from sleep.

I had listened to the evening news. The forecast was for below-freezing temperatures in the night. I was staying in a white frame house fifty miles from the Columbus airport on a narrow and winding road. A grandchild, due February 5, was coming early. I had a 7:50 a.m. flight. I had not driven that particular road before. I did not know the Columbus airport.

That morning, in the continuing wind, I heard a noise I knew was the crack of a tree limb falling to the ground. I knew it was ice breaking the branch. The frame house is near a wooded area. I wondered if the electricity would go off. I thought of the flashlight on the night table beside my bed. I continued to prepare to leave in the middle of the night to an airport where I'd only been once before, when I'd been dropped off by a driver on a previous trip to Kenyon College. Now I was driving by myself over the wet road that could be icy in places. But once on the road, I saw the lights of the highway department truck spreading salt.

On the trip to the airport, four days after my arrival in Ohio, I traveled at a slow pace. A few other cars came up from behind and passed. I checked the map in the headlight in the car. 229, 161, 270, 670, the airport. Where to park? I saw cars turning left in the dark. I followed. There in the long-term parking, I took out my bags in the cold. I made my way to a waiting van for a ride to the airport. I was going to Texas for the birth of a grandchild, my fourth, but the first from my son, who is forty-three. It has been a long wait for his child. A boy, Ray, would be born January 18, 2008. The only child they would have, my daughter-in-law told me. She had had a rough pregnancy, and now the birth would be a few weeks early because of her health.

How often I have started out into the darkness on a wet road in the cold, not knowing where I was going? It must be something like new parents must feel, if I remembered correctly. I had stopped by the security office after classes the day before, and they drew a map for me. I had driven through blizzards the years I lived in Minnesota. I knew I had made it through worse weather. I knew I could make it through snow.

The day before, I called my daughter to tell her of the impending birth. I could hear the noise of my three grandchildren in the background. It was a snow day, she said. I knew the turmoil of three small children. It was with guilt I left Kansas City to teach at Kenyon College for a semester.

I had retired from teaching in 2005 to move to Kansas City to be near by daughter and grandchildren because I wanted to be part of their lives. I had been commuting seven hours from St. Paul anyway. I decided it was time to retire from the small college where I had been. I left with some regret to spend two years without teaching. Now I had returned. If I was still in Kansas City, I could easily have driven the nine-hour trip to Rhome, Texas, just northwest of Fort Worth, where my son and daughter-in-law live.

After the flight, I took the shuttle to the rental cars, and drove sixty miles from the DFW airport to the hospital in Decatur, Texas. I arrived at 11:30 a.m. I sat in her room most of the day with my son and some of her family. The monitor beeped the baby's heart beat and my daughter's-in-law contractions. In late afternoon, the doctor felt the baby would be born my C-section, but decided to give the induced labor a while longer. By 11:00 that evening, my daughter-in-law went to surgery. Ray was born at 11:57 p.m.

I left the hospital around 1:00 a.m. to drive from Decatur to my son's house in Rhome, a trip of probably twenty-five minutes in the bright moonlight of a Texas night. I turned down the gravel road off the highway and parked in the yard of his house and left the car lights shining toward the front door as I unloaded my rental car. The cold front that had dipped into the country had reached as far as Texas. It probably was twenty-five degrees by then.

The next morning I was at the hospital early. I rang the bell to the delivery area, but was told my daughter-in-law could not have visitors because she was exhausted and needed the day to rest. My son was then on the cell phone saying that he would stay with his wife. I thought of the baby in his rollable bed in the nursery alone. This new grandchild had wanted to suck after birth, but instead of comfort, I listened to his cries as he was given an IV with antibiotics because his mother had developed a fever during labor.

As I sat in the waiting room by myself, I felt like that branch fallen from a tree in the woods near the white frame house in Gambier. It is a lockout that contemporary medicine has come to, though to be fair, it also can mean survival for mother and child.

If labor could be called anything pleasant, it could be called at least nearly painless, as my daughter-in-law often was unaware of the contractions that passed on the monitor. It would be the next days, probably the next weeks that she would feel the pain and the slow recovery from her ordeal.

The baby's doctor said the baby's kidneys were enlarged. He would have to go to a specialist. My son and daughter-in-law asked me to make the return trip the next week and I would, because I was asked to come, and because I wanted to, even though I could only stay three days each time I came. My daughter-in-law had lost her mother through cancer. One relative was taking care of my daughter's-in-law grandmother. The other relative worked. I would read my assignments on the plane to prepare for classes when I returned. I would be there with my new grandchild, as I had the others. A family meant connection and inclusion, and I would not accept the cold I felt.

T(ravel)

I decided to drive to the Scissortail Conference in Ada, Oklahoma, to which I had been invited, though it was a thousand miles from Gambier.

The Monday night before I left, a student to my left in class coughed the entire time. It is a three-hour workshop. We sit together around a table. I thought of asking him to leave, but decided not do. It wasn't long before I felt the disruption in my nose. The sensitivity to breath. The sneezing.

I have a small cabin in the Missouri Ozarks. My sister-in-law sells real estate, and found it for me. I had a lot of work done. Walls painted, rugs stripped, a laminate wood floor put in, a screened in porch across the front, a tree-house for the grandchildren. The man who built the porch said that my cabin looked like a baseball cap, the porch being the bill of the round cap.

On the news, I saw the clouds that covered central plains to Ohio, which they call the Midwest, though it looks east on the map to me. On Thursday mornings, I have a 9:40 to 11:00 class, which I let out half an hour early. I was on the road shortly after. It takes two hours to get from Gambier to I-70 west of Columbus. In Indiana, and then Illinois, I saw the water standing in fields. I saw the swollen creeks and rivers. I wondered if I would make it to the cabin because of my tiredness, and sickness, but in western Illinois, just east of St. Louis, where planes landed and took off over Lambert Field, I saw vapor trails in the evening sky, backlit by the setting sun. They made several large crosses in the air before me. Then it was dark, and I saw only the headlights on the road ahead. About 9:00 p.m. I arrived at my cabin in the Ozarks.

When I stepped in the door, I knew the throw-rug was wet. There was water on my new floors and mud along the walls. I got towels and cleaned it up. My cabin sits on the lake. There is a steep hill behind it. The rain came down the hill, across the road, and down into the drive, spilling mud over the rock wall onto the steps down to my cabin and into the cabin.

My face throbbed from my cold and sore throat. I still had the sneezing and coughing in the early stages of a cold as I cleaned up the rainwater and mud in my house.

I sat on the edge of my bed that night in my familiar room and prayed. I always ask the Lord to protect my cabin. I think the damage was minimal. I would have to have some work done. I'll have to find someone to dig a drainage ditch and reinforce the wall to divert the water.

I also wondered how I was going to read at the conference when I could hardly talk. But my way seemed easy. I was not persecuted. I was not thrown to the lions. I could live my life holding on to what I could imagine was my own. I knew it when I read the Bible. I recognized something beyond myself. Something at stake that I wanted to be a part of.

When I bought my cabin in the Ozarks, the old ramp to the dock was rotting, and I had to have it replaced. The workers had trouble aligning the new ramp and the dock to the concrete block that anchored it. That day, there were other workers clearing some brush from the side of the lake road. The dock workers borrowed their caterpillar and moved the concrete block for alignment. In the few years since, I have noticed the block turning up, tilting toward the lake. The dock slowly may be pulling the heavy block into the lake. Owning property is the continual process of upkeep and repair. Maintenance is the measuring rod of a nation, as the longshoreman, Eric Hoffer, once said. Scripture for me is maintenance, though, as the years go by, I feel the pull of the concrete block to the edge of the lake.

I was thinking Christianity would be easier, and I waited, and waited, and am still waiting, and am changed while I am waiting for what change I thought change was. But God's change does not seem to be my idea of change. Our ideas are different. What change did I want? To suffer less. To be more certain. I wanted to love church more instead of the times I feel attendance by duty. Nothing would move me. Nothing would reach the core of where I was with help. But you continue breathing, though the self has left part of itself behind. And there is a ripped place, an opening that lets in the weather, whether cold or hot, snow or rain, tornado or stillness. It seems even earthquake is weather. And you have cried from your stomach in jumps, as if out of breath, as if you have been running a long time with a rhythm of waves that will never stop pushing the shore, and backpulling the dock from the land. You can write about it now from this distance in time and space. In the half moon, you see the curved shore as if a bay, not a sharp outline, but dull, and it will come back and back and there is nothing you can do. The steadiness of it is your foothold.

In the morning, I felt better. I continued my drive to Oklahoma. I would stay away from people with my cold. I would give my reading at a distance and leave. Travel is a sacred space inside my car when I am alone and on a long trip.

The Mound Builders

> I've always cherished solitude. | Stéphane Mallarmé, "Autumn Lament," from *Divagations*

Saturday was chilly, cloudy, wet. It wasn't a day for travel, but I wanted to visit the Indian mounds in southern Ohio, and it was the last weekend I had before I left Kenyon College at the end of the 2008 semester. I had found them on the map—the Mounds City Group, the Hopewell Mound Group, the Hopeton Earthworks, the Seip Earthworks between Bourneville and Bainbridge, and the Serpent Mound near Peebles. I wanted to travel because everything is still ahead in travel. In travel, I drive from here to there. I achieve destination. Travel is a process of learning.

I was teaching an Essay as Literature course that semester. We were ending with Mallarmé's *Divagations*, which means digressions, or wanderings. It was a distant, difficult book, written in French, translated into English in a process that seemed impossible. It also was a long book. How does anyone translate abstractions with an interplay of sound relationships that don't exist in the language in which it is translated? But in *Divagations*, Mallarmé wanted to depict not the thing, but the effect it produced—the same way, I think, that the Indians wanted to produce their effect—evoking the same indirect method—not merely describing, but making a new object out of the indirectness.

THE MOUND BUILDERS

The Kokosing River, near Gambier, which is more of a creek, was high in its banks, like other streams and rivers after the weeks of rain. Water stood in low places in the fields. I drove through rolling hills and the clumps of woods between the fields — past white farmhouses, barns, outbuildings, and a single farm wagon by the road. There were purple flowers in the edges of fields — clover, I suppose. I thought the hills must be where the Mound Builders got their idea to build mounds.

The mounds stretch along Ohio roads — SRs — "State Routes" are what they are called — from Newark, just south of Gambier, to Chillicothe, to Peebles, some 150 miles from Gambier — along 37, 159, 50, 41, 73 — I carried the pieces of *Divagations* with me — Everything is suspended, an arrangement of fragments with alternations and confrontations — from the section "Crisis of Verse."

Some two thousand years ago in the Ohio Valley, the Indians dug with sticks and clamshells and stone hoes. They carried the earth in baskets to build the mounds. Maybe the mounds were built according to astronomical observations, the solstice or equinox. Maybe they were simple burial mounds. Maybe they served more than one purpose — some built for one reason, others built for another. Much of it remains a mystery. But there seems to be a mathematical relationship — The mounds seem to be built in a grid along waterways — There seems to be an alignment to sun, to stars, to one another. There seems to be some invisible connection between them. They also seem to connect to other mounds I have visited — Spiro in eastern Oklahoma, Cahokia in western Illinois on the Mississippi River, the mounds above the Mississippi River in St. Paul, Minnesota, where I used to live, and the mounds on the Missouri River near Kansas City, where I live now.

At the Hopewell Culture National Historical Park in Chillicothe, I learned that the Hopewell Indians were named after Mr. Hopewell, the farmer on whose property the mounds were first excavated in 1890s by Warren K. Moorehead. The original artifacts are in the British National Museum. The replicas are in the interpretive center near Chillicothe — Copper needle and bone awl. Copper bear and antlers for ceremonial headdresses. Copper hands. A copper peregrine falcon. Copper stars. Many small stone effigies, most of them used for pipes.

The mounds contained mica, obsidian, copper, flint, pipestone, and shells from a trade network that spanned the North American continent.

I stood at the exhibit of the charnel house, a building in which dead bodies were placed. I read the information about the ceremonies.

I also read that some of the Hopewell mounds at Chillicothe had been leveled for Fort Sherman, a World War I training camp. Farming and looting had leveled other mounds. I wondered if the soldiers at Fort Sherman had any sense of what their barracks sat upon, or if they felt the past move under them at night as they dreamed.

Every time I am at my small cabin in the Lake of the Ozarks in Missouri, a few more wooded acres have been bulldozed for development. I see the industrialization of landscape, the acculturation of landscape, one thing becoming another and remaining little of itself. It had its beginning in the mound builders, always excavating in one place, accumulating in another, even Mallarme was a mound builder, moving language around. All those *alternations* I felt moving under me in travel. Even time alternates. Sometimes when I am at the lake, I hear the lake woods as it was. I receive an image of what it was like when I was a child. When the past floats like a paper doll dress.

All that day, I drove roads that curved back and forth through the country, finding one mound after another. Sometimes they were hard to determine — They seemed lost and insignificant among other hills. Other times, they were definite, such as the Seip mounds. It seemed to me the Indians followed the natural terrain in their patterns. Maybe they were after process rather than the mounds themselves. Maybe in the end, it was not the mounds that were the focus, but the alignment of their work to the land. Maybe the Indians worked arranging their own patterns in accordance to the patterns they saw around them. Sven Birkerts speaks also of this sameness in his book on nonfiction, *The Art of Time in Memoir: Then, Again:* "I discerned the possibility of hidden patterns, patterns that, if unearthed and understood, would somehow explain me — my life — to myself."

Reading a review of *Divagations* by Evlyn Gould at the University of Oregon, "Penciling and Erasing Mallarme's Ballets," she explained how ballet is in the nature of writing:

> But the essay, like all of Mallarme's writing, also comes complete with its own deconstructive voice to which one may choose to listen, carefully. The hidden mobility of these voices creates the choreographic allure of the essay by surrounding apparently singular images with the petals of only virtual blossoms, an imaginary corps de ballet encircling the stars; their poetry is only "heard" or "envisioned" as one reads. And as one reads, so many of Mallarme's sentences dance on, puffing themselves up with relative clauses, that the relatives become more captivating than the sense of the whole they mobilize and detail in fractions, infinitely. This turns reading into translation, a continual exercise in penciling and erasing no different from what dancers do as they write in space.

Often, writing seems to work as dreams work. As dance works. We need Mallarme's difficulties — the subconscious renderings of experience. We spend so much time in sleep, the way the mind works in dreams has to be important, too. Dreams serve many purposes of arranging, edifying, sorting, developing. There is something in us that works in a dreamlike way. That longs for something other than logic and order. Maybe the "puffs" of mounds strung out across the earth were the dreams of the Indians. Or maybe they represented their necessary "mobility." Line dancing with a convincing otherness. I think we work during sleep. Sometimes I wake in the morning with further thoughts on something I'd been working on.

Mallarme's *Divagations* is a significant book. It is abstract, nonlinear. It separates language from itself until it becomes something other than itself. Instead of a tool for communication, it becomes idea. It is an intense book that vivifies creative nonfiction. How fortunate for nonfiction, which now calls itself the fourth genre, that it can circle back and pick up Pliny, St. Augustine, Montaigne, Pascal, Mallarmé, who all, to some extent, worked in peripheral and experimental fields, accumulating their experiences into a mound.

Finally, I reached Serpent Mound. I parked, walked through the interpretive center, and was shown the way to the serpent. I climbed the scaffolding, where I looked down on the serpent. I also saw that the mound was as winding as the creek at the bottom of the hill. It was winding as the roads I had driven. Maybe the Indians had watched a migrating herd meandering through the valley, and copied their trail. The Serpent Mound was not an exact copy of a snake. It was not a duplicate, but more the idea of winding — of a link to something beyond it, whatever its meaning.

I think in the same way, it wasn't the text of the mounds, or the serpent, or the winding river or undulating hills, or migrating animals the Indians watched in the valley feeding as they walked — but it was the process of the journey — serpentine, meandering — moving which serpent mound certainly was, though it didn't move. But movement was there in the undulating, raised earth ridge that from the nearby scaffolding or platform could be seen as *serpent*. Maybe the serpent was an emblem. To do, to act, to make, to shape, to be. It was what I was after on my journey that day. Maybe the essay is a mound builder—A place for artifice. Or maybe the mounds are an essay. To take a danger and shape it. To tame Ou'Wash.

How fortunate Ohio can go back and access its mound history, the way the essay can go back and pick up its ancestry.

I am a stranger on earth. Much of what I should have been is lost. I have known defeat, violation, isolation. Sometimes there is such longing, or sometimes an anger in me, especially when I see the Indian people as artifact, named for a farmer who lived on their land centuries later, their original artifices in the British Museum. How much removal and erasure, yet the essence is there—in the land, and in the voices on the land if you stand there in the rain long enough. If you don't give up—if you continue in travel—

This work of shaping, of doing, of being in the moving place where it is possible *to be*.

In May 2009, I was in London for performances of my play *Salvage* at Riverside Studios during an Origins Festival. I went to the British Museum, and there in a case by themselves were the effigies from the Ohio mounds. I saw the small deer antlers. I saw the toad, frog, and otter. I saw the bird effigy with sad eyes. There were shell gorgets. A copper axe blade. Adze. There was an explanation the artifacts were found in several of the mounds along the Scioto River in Ross County, three miles north of Chillicothe, Ohio. There was a photograph of the Serpent Mound with a remark that it was carbon dated at 1070 AD. There was information about punctuate design—fragments of small sandstone tablets carved with rattlesnakes. It was a small but decent-sized room, given the small number of Native Americans in relationship to the world's populations. There were display cases of other Native American cultures around the walls, and several cases standing in the middle, one of which contained the Ohio mound artifacts that had made their journey across the ocean. I thought about the boxing, packing, crating of the artifacts, their shipment possibly first by wagon, then train, and finally a ship along the waterway of a different kind.

The Shape of Privacy

In Texas—these mornings I wake in my son's house, before I pick up the baby. I am by myself in the shape of privacy, which is memory. It comes like St. Augustine says, "certain things come forth immediately . . . some rooted in deeper receptacles." It is true—some memories rush back, out of order, others seem in order, with various reasons and purposes for becoming these mounds of memory. All of them seemingly and somehow knocked loose by associations. This morning, I remember making my mother unhappy by causing trouble one evening and being put out on the front porch in the darkness where, in the streetlight, I saw a neighbor walking up the street, and I moved behind the post trying to hide so as not to be seen in my transgression. I think now he saw me, but he didn't act like he did.

It was out there in the broken field of memory, dug into with the shell of memory, gathered in a basket of memory, taken to a mound to shape the memory of the unruliness I had been given. For some reason, it takes a broken field to understand.

Later in the week, in the Kimbell Museum in Fort Worth, I stood at a table reading *Self Portrait in a Velvet Dress*, Frida Kahlo Memoria, 1937. The book, published by Chronicle Books, San Francisco, was photographs of Frida's wardrobe from the Museo Frida Kahlo. Several photos were paintings Frida had made of dresses on hangers with herself in the foreground—*aanii, aanii,* those were her clothes.

What difference does sorting through the self make? What difference, our paper dresses? Our clothes on their hangers? Our closets? Our little mounds? What difference, this narrative nonfiction, literary nonfiction, creative nonfiction, these *reportages*, these *factuals* dressed in cutout patterns, this frontier of nonfictional writing?

As I move toward the end of a book, I feel the next one coming. It starts to get pebbly and I know I should let it go. But when do I cut it off? What about the overlaps? I never know where a book ends. They all are given in a gnarl. Writing has been an act of ungnarling. As I try to finish, I look back over the beginning. If I could, I would lift the rock from these pages and watch her [M(other)'s] unhappiness float away like paper doll dresses in the wind.

One Who Wears Moths

> There are rivers, superhighways of energy... and there are junctions where they meet. | Sam Shaw, *Run Like Fire Once More*

It seems to me there are mark lines across the earth — something like fault lines that are not fractures but *continuancies*. They are bindings that hold together. They are road lines that serve as preservations of what already has passed and disappeared. Yet the relics are here — invisible markings like longitude and latitude that travel the earth. Marking one thing to another in a peripheral way, usually not direct sight, but off there in the field I pass are the *runnings* to other places. Preservations that leave minimal evidences of what can be surmised or guessed at. The mark lines are the voices of the earth. The roadways of landscape. The through-lines of its *transcendency*. A *landscript* that marks the land. They are like the invisible lines that hold the constellations into the figures they are called by. Sometimes I think they are *bawl* lines — when I feel sorrow traversing the atmosphere. Those bindings around the earth always evident in travel.

Over the 2009 spring break from school, I drove 445 miles from Gambier, Ohio, to Boone, North Carolina. I gave a talk at Appalachian State University, and went to bed. I woke around 2:00 a.m. to start the 924-mile journey to Kansas City, where I live most of the time, and where I have grandchildren. When I wake with the road calling, I go. I was going to drive halfway, maybe over halfway, but when I called my daughter, the children had a program at school that evening to which I was invited. I kept going. I arrived in Kansas City just after 5:00 p.m. Fifteen hours of passing through the space just above the road.

Sometimes when traveling to one place, another place comes through. Sometimes there is an overlay of voices from other times. Voices carry the earth. Therefore, the land is an act of memory.

Two days after my long journey of returning to Kansas City for spring break, I had a trip to read from my work at the University of North Dakota in Grand Forks. I watched the weather for another blizzard up there. But it looked clear for a few days. I looked online at airfares, but travel to a place off the usual travel lanes was expensive: $600 to $1,100. I decided to drive. I knew the air crossed above me with planes. Just look at the vapor trails. Each day there is a network of planes crossing north–south, east–west, northeast–southeast, northwest–southwest, and crosswise across the sky along their set routes. They often follow the interstates, or use the highways for navigation. The blots of cities are markers too. I imagined the diagonal lines — lines circling back upon themselves. All of them still there in unrecognizable forms. Destinations toward which the highways are headed, toward which they connect in an overall movement that has nothing to do with destination, but in the movement itself. The journey is the process of journey. The gathering of moth wings until one can fly.

I know these trails north into the cold — I-35 and I-29 up through Iowa, Minnesota, the Dakotas. These interstates patchy with ice. Sometimes one lane. Sometimes two tracks. I know the noise of the car over ruts in the ice. The slight slippage of wheels as the car shifts before finding its placement [footing] again. There are 282 miles alone between Sioux Falls, South Dakota, and Fargo, North Dakota. At times I drive 25 miles an hour in a 75-mile-an-hour speed limit. The snowplow ahead mainly butts the snow — packs it on the road sometimes — pressing it like a fork on the rim of a pie plate. From 9 degrees it went up to 10 degrees, then 11 degrees at midday, and back down as I drove north past Fargo to Grand Forks ninety miles from the Canadian border. Sometimes a storm misses certain sections of the interstate and for miles the highway is clear — but the road ahead has a mirage of ice always receding as I travel toward it. The road in the distance looks as though I should expect ice, but when I reach the place, the road is dry. The mirage of ice is thin streams of snow blowing across the road. Or the salt the highway department spreads during blizzards turns to powder when the road dries — and a car passing lifts a thin veil of salt from the road. I watch the white fields with their rows of stubble and the ice-crusted creeks. In places where the sky is clear, a vapor trail spreads like a fish skeleton with rows of thin bones on either side of the spine. I remember 117 degrees on the dashboard thermometer as I passed Yuma last summer on the Arizona–southern California border. The cold draws patterns on the side windows and the edges of the windshield the defrost doesn't reach. It is marriage to careful attendance. If you have it down cold, you have it. If you are cold on the trail, you don't have it at all. I like these words going opposite ways at once, the way opposite lanes of the interstates move across the country. Several days later, I would wake with the thought: I am in a machine that is dying, wobbling and soon disappearing under me, I fly over the handlebars and continue on. I think of the red dirt roads of Oklahoma and central Australia. The land is a *continu-ness* with flags of water between.

    After the program at UND, I make the 689-mile return from Grand Forks to Kansas City, Missouri, where I would have the last week of spring break with my grandchildren.

    The land edifies the concept of the time it fractures. How comprehensible the horizon when I recognize the form of mark lines upon it. The rhetorical cast of the trees. The flocking of snow in the field. The wool is spacious. Or is it the snow? The serrated strips of road over the ice. Black energy. The big rip. The forces at work against it. Not to destroy, but to change according to the migrations of the mark lines, which are different from our trails. Alone on the road that follows glacial ruts and animal migrations, I feel the voracity of modality—that tracking of a predator that seeks patterns from the past. The hunger of its world. The rhetoric of a car going on a road. The *going* as a noun, a process, an object of momentum. The mark-lines of roads I have seen from a plane.

This is what I hear in the cold. This is what I feel crossing the trap lines. Speech lines of wind patterns, indentions from animal paths, primitive migrations, the trails of explorers and wagons. Currents of motion. Even ocean currents that primitive people followed long before Marco Polo and Columbus.

There are acts of agency on the road still serrated with ice in the good weather they tell me they are having in Grand Forks. Indeed, the trip was a respite between blizzards that eventually, once again, flooded the Red River that flows north into Canada.

The cold is a presence. If it were visible, it would have knives for fingers and fierce white eyes. It would have a sharp beak. It is a carnivore. How did anyone survive in a sod house on the open prairie? The cold is hostile territory. It is the ghost of old glaciers that once inhabited the land. Maybe still do at this time of year. It comes to overrun. To take into itself. It is One-who-makes-a-web. One-who-makes-its-breath-marks-to-show. One-who-wears-moths.

There is a moth quality to the cold. It seems dusty. Powdery. It seems fragile with transparent wings. "Moths watched us through the window"—Adam Zagajewski says in his poem "Moths." But I think it is us who watch them.

This from a program on *All Things Considered*, August 18, 2007, which I found on Wikipedia:

"Moths frequently appear to circle artificial lights. One

hypothesis advanced to explain this behavior is that moths use a technique of celestial navigation called transverse orientation. By maintaining a constant angular relationship to a bright celestial light, such as the moon, they can fly in a straight line. Celestial objects are so far away, that even after travelling great distances, the change in angle between the moth and the light source is negligible; further, the moon will always be in the upper part of the visual field or on the horizon. When a moth encounters a much closer artificial light and uses it for navigation, the angle changes noticeably after only a short distance, in addition to being often below the horizon. The moth instinctively attempts to correct by turning toward the light, causing airborne moths to come plummeting downward... which results in a spiral flight path that gets closer and closer to the light source."

The transparent trace lines I often find on the road are the distant light source of my travel. They are a necessary *oftenness* I find on the road. Not the old, *we are drawn to the light* business, but a new thought wave of travel. Maybe it's one of the reasons for my *goings* on the roads. To gain distance. To reach the connectives that are in the *goings*. They are there hitchhiking. I don't even have to stop and they're in the car, riding there beside me. Trying to take the wheel.

By the time I drove 750 miles from Kansas City back to Gambier, Ohio, after spring break, I had driven 3,961 miles: Gambier OH, to Boone NC, to Kansas City, to Grand Forks ND, to Kansas City, to Gambier OH.

> The birds/gather thickly around that outcrop/of trees: fill the laneway with traffic | John Kinsella, "Canto of the Mound of Earth," from *Divine Comedy*

There are lane ways on the earth. Lane marks that become roads that become highways that become interstates that become the road lines that traverse. Who knows what really is there beneath them? How much imagined? How much known? Base lines. Space lines. These *moundings* rebuilt for passage. These thought lines that flutter like moths. They hardly have time to land.

Sometimes when I see the full moon, it seems like the moon is transparent. The marks in the moon are from something behind it. The light of the moon seems a gauze through which something else shows. Boxes of some sort stacked up. Some sort of cargo waiting for delivery. Sometimes when I travel, I see the transparency of the earth. It's like watching the stirrings of dust motes floating in a shaft of sunlight from the window of a room. The motes are places under the vast open air of our country. The relational patterns of the motes to space and the separation lines between them are evident.

Are not the salt plains of northern Oklahoma the old ocean that dried up? What is it I heard driving there? *The ocean is upset. It's not itself. What is it grumbling about? What a grouch. It's tied up in a corral I can't see. I'm corralled with voices. The whole earth rolled into a ball of twine lines.*

Often, it's the evaporated parts I hear:

> Four boys who escaped from the reform school at Jamesburg, New Jersey, several weeks ago, and tramped two of the coldest nights of this winter, are crippled for life. Their hands and feet were badly frozen. Tuesday it became necessary to cut off five of the eight frozen feet. Three of the boys lost a foot each, and one boy lost two. | *The Indian Helper*, Carlisle Indian School Newspaper, Friday, February 7, 1896

Voices I have read are picked up in the travel lines. They float along in the energy trail of those who have picked up on them, of those in whose knowledge they dwell.

Often I hear the voices of those who did not have a chance to speak. Sometimes that hearing takes place along the baselines of sound that is heard while moving. Otherwise the information becomes like the cold. It is where schools often go wrong, mainly boarding schools of the past. They made learning difficult — sometimes impossible for someone along different baselines. They presented learning that bypassed natural ways of hearing that was meant to cause understanding. They bypassed necessary concept lines and set up an adversarial position.

The continents also travel with voices of the mark lines. They are like the wings of moths. They direct the places of our other shores. After traveling long distances, I feel pasted with visages of wings. The point is achieving connectives to another. The transverse multiplicities of the mark lines.

> Long time, olden time, no white people bin here. Nothing. Only Napperby Station, that way, and Hermannsburg. That's all. My father traveled from here, he traveled north, right up Hermannsburg. Him gettn blanket, clothes, bush knife, and axe, there. Him go back. You know, olden people, long time ago, they bin walking around everyway. Everyway. | Dinny Japaljarri, Warlpiri, Yuendumu, August 9, 1977, in *Long Time, Olden Time: Aboriginal Accounts of Northern Territory History*

I need to be on the road alone to hear the passageways. To remember the passages I've read. The old journeys — all of them gone. But preserved in a way that looks nothing like them.

Often in travel I cover my ears. I wear ear muffs when continents join and the voices grow too loud. There are modalities of travel contextualized in the elements. Old course lines such as the coursing of wind through the trees slanting them a certain way. A variableness in the roof lines of the trees. I think of trails of ants. I think of the termite mounds I saw in Australia. The following of geese after one another marked by their trails in the air. There are times I drive long distances. I don't always mean to, but it happens, and I am drawn along on one of those lines. I hear them in sleep. I wake to a venatic journey. Voices hunt the earth. They actually carry the earth.

These voices sandbag the threat of flood during travel. I have to get in the car from time to time and drive great distances. Running from self. From duties. From presence. To look for the light on the moon from which to navigate. To get away. To get near. Always these contradictory lanes going opposite ways.

Here it is—the little car into which I have to step, and it is pushed from the shore to travel by itself, in this life anyway, and it's my job to make the isolation interesting—to steer the car without oars between icebergs, between whales, until it goes into the dark cold water that is my sea. I travel the sullen road where I have to keep from sinking though I already am gone into it—I have to break the sea into pieces. To call its drowning an interstate. To float in the indirectness of an angular relationship. To know the great mystery of the interstates: the roads are water. The waves fall upon themselves to make the wet places and ice strips smaller and smaller to pass over. The Jaunts. Junkets. Jumps. Jibes. Jives. Journeys. Jobs.

... crushed before the moth—Job 4:19, ... eaten by the moth—Job 13:28, corrupted by the moth—Matthew 6:19, Mark 6:20, and Luke 12:33.

I will be ... like a moth—Hosea 5:12. I am the moth in my own wool. How often I use my artificial light to land.

He builds his house like a moth—Job 27:18. I build the self-constructed travel on the idea of memory. *They bin* [driving] *long time ago.*

Until finally, "... consumed like the moth"—Psalm 39:11.

I follow old haunt-lines. I am something I was maybe before

birth and will be again on the other side of this life, which is passage along the Maker's trace lines, differentiated by development and transformation.

> Blessed be the Gasoline.
> Blessed be the Road.
> Blessed be our Savior and our Truth.

At the Methodist church in the village of Gambier, Ohio, which is just the college campus of sixteen hundred students, a post office, a few stores along Middle Path, and an assortment of outlying houses, twenty-five at most attend on a Sunday morning. On Maundy Thursday, I go to the evening Holy Thursday service. A table is set for the last supper. Eleven of us are at the table.

I feel the icy wind of my thoughts that will not be quiet, that will not quit their driving a hundred miles away. The stained glass windows giving off their travels in the evening light pull me onward. The sad terror before the cross catches me in the warplines of the gospel. I feel my moth-eaten heart. How is Christ the one who wears moths? Why do I feel his tarp lines? Why does a humble Christ come to me as the one who wears moths? In the cold where I lived, and in the heat through which I have traveled at other times. He is the one on a long journey to gather believers. He comes dragging his trap lines. He wants us on his road of endurance, his long haul. Jesus died in the snow, trying to be the light of navigation for his little moths flopping around without him. Trying to take the significance of his act away from myself to him, whom I should recognize as the Christ, the Road and the Way. Faith seems fragile as the moon. As a moth wing. As a vapor spot in the sky.

> Go into the city, and there you will meet a man bearing a pitcher of water; follow him ... wherever he goes in, say to the owner of the house ... where is the guest room? ... and he will show you a large upper room, furnished and prepared. | Mark 14:13–15

The man carrying a pitcher of water is a mystery. Christ had others who knew he was having a last supper? He had more than we know? The preparers of the table? The leaders to the way? He asks that I set down my cargo. He presents his shadow puppets behind a screen. I see the transparency of the moon, the earth, everything drifting without Christ.

After Jesus' arrest, they lit a fire in the courtyard and were seated together — Luke 22:55. A woman looked "earnestly" at Peter and said, "This man was also with him." Peter starts his engine and flees into the cold.

I like the domesticity of the Bible — the barrel fire, the difficulty of carrying a bowl of water. No, it was a pitcher.

What is this journey through language? These words? This essay/nonfiction form? This democratization of literature? This reality show? This new western frontier where everyone has a gun? This dispensation with its disputed *edgings*? These wrap lines across the stripes of cold? Or heat? Or the extremes of both?

How do you shape these varying parts together? This genre in which the narrator reveals his/her ragged little voice, and the subject or event exposes its voice as it turns over and over in the narrator's hands with a transcendence into meaning somewhere near the end. This new form of writing intrudes into the literary genres of fiction, poetry, drama, is an aliquant part, leaving itself as a remainder, as not yet qualified, dignified, adopted into the big leagues, but so far awkwardly making room for itself, edging others out, as a matter of fact, in the marketing of a written product.

Last summer, for another research trip and workshop, I left Decatur, Texas, northwest of Fort Worth, after dinner in a Mexican café, saying good-bye to my son, daughter-in-law, and grandson.

After dark, on I-20 between Abilene and Sweet Water, the lightning began — Fingers of lightning. Outstretched hands of lightning.

The sky so bright sometimes I could see the dark cloud-swirls of a Van Gogh sky. I felt the wind buffet the car. The sky was angry. It was going to pound whatever/whoever was in its way. Highway signs shimmied. Then the wind, dirt, stubble, straws, tumbleweed blew from the north across the road. I felt the car wanting to go with them.

Cars pulled off the road. The wind battered all that was not tied down. The lightning continued from the dark clouds like a switch quickly turned on and off, as if signifying the second act about to start. It was going to be a maelstrom. I also saw trucks pull off the road. I saw truckers tightening the ropes on their rigs. Ahead, I saw a rise in the interstate and knew there was a road under it. Maybe a road where cars could cross under the highway because, once in a while, they have to get from here to there across the Texas plains. How else to do it with an interstate in the way?

I left the highway on the access road, past trucks also stopped, and found the place under the raised part of the interstate. It was not a road for cars, but an underpass under the highway. I turned into it, then turned around so that I faced the storm. Maybe half an hour the storm raged. The gusts of wind bullied my car. It seemed to lift and fall as if revving for a quick start in a street race. I kept my foot on the brake as though it would hold the car in place. Then everything grew light. A bright light was coming? Had I been blown away in the storm? Was this the afterlife? The light swirled around the car in the wind—and another sound—a train-sound grew—I was sure I was still alive under the highway. The bright light was on a train engine coming into view behind me. The opening under the highway was an angular crossing for the train tracks I had not seen. I had stopped in an underpass for a train. It passed close to the car. If I had pulled back any further, I would have been on the tracks. But I would have felt the tracks under the car, even in the dark, and would have known what was there. It was a long train. I held my foot on the brake now as if to prevent the wind from blowing me back into it. It was hot in the car. But if I tried to lower the window, the wind and rain swept in.

Even in the disruption of the storm, I felt the steady shape-lines holding still.

Afterward, I drove energized by the storm. I stopped at a rest stop just after midnight but could not rest. I drove another hour or two and stopped again. When I put the backseat down in my car, I can lie down. My head against the driver's seat, my feet against the back gate of the car. I slept off and on a few hours with the noise of the traffic, the lightning that still ruled the sky, and the buffets of wind still shoving the car.

Before dawn, I drove again across the barren Texas land until I could see the drilling rigs for oil and natural gas. The bleakness. The ugliness. I-20 to I-10 and eventually I-8. I felt sleep coming like a storm, and stopped at another rest stop and slept from 6:00 to 8:00 a.m., then drove again. How can anyone drive 600 miles and still be in Texas?

In the light, I saw the dirt and bits of straw stuck to the front of the car. I should have turned the car away from the storm, the way horses turn their backs to the wind.

In El Paso, I turned off the interstate. I remembered a downtown art gallery I had visited years ago but couldn't find it. El Paso was grim as I sat at a stoplight at the bus station, when there is no work in Mexico that sends the immigrants across the border in all that rising sand in which their dreams must stir. Are they supposed to stand as a sideboard to their lives and watch it pass without hope?

That night, I stopped at Willcox, Arizona. At 5:00 the next morning, I walked near the motel. The desert was scorched by the sun as soon as it came up, but the sand was made to live in the intense heat.

In Yuma, a thermometer at a gas station said 108 degrees, though on the interstate, my dashboard thermometer registered 117 degrees. Maybe it was the heat from the road or the engine.

In the desert I saw trains of at least a hundred cars, piggyback, coming from the ports in San Diego east across the country. The whole land felt like an overdone meatloaf as the temperature continued to rise crossing southern New Mexico and Arizona into California toward San Diego. From time to time, whirlwinds of dust lifted from the flat desert. Rising columns of sand. Disturbances in the mark lines traveling. There are signs along the road, "Zero visibility is possible. Do not stop in the lanes of traffic." There are names like Calexico, El Centro, Plaster City, Ocotillo, Jacumba. There are border patrols and exits to border crossings. The starkness of the sand dunes. The mountains that looked like rock piles as I started into them. They seemed like a crowd of people standing there — maybe waiting for their loaves and fish by the Sea of Galilee.

"Woe to him that says . . . to the dumb stone, Arise . . . there is no breath at all in it"—Habakkuk 2:19. Yet the stones can testify against someone doing something wrong: "The stone will cry out of the wall"—Habakkuk 2:11. In other places in scripture, the stones will cry out in praise: In Luke 19:40, the Pharisees complain that the disciples are praising Jesus on his triumphal entry into Jerusalem. Christ tells them, "If these should hold their peace, the stones would immediately cry out." These massive, rounded boulders along I-8 seemed living. Silent, but living. Bless these interstates through the Bible going their opposite ways.

From sea level, I-8 climbed 1,000 to 2,000 to 3,000 to 4,000 feet across Tricate Divide, elevation 4,140 feet. There were signs warning of falling rock. There were other signs warning to turn off air conditioners when climbing the steep lanes up the mountains. I didn't push the car. It slowed sometimes to nearly stopping at the summits while other cars rushed by. I passed a few trucks and cars with their hoods up, pulled off the road. I saw two boys with their cell phones, waiting for someone to come for them, their old car refusing to go further, pushed beyond endurance. Afterward, I went down and down into the San Diego basin.

Notes from the Observatory

He counts the number of the stars. He calls them all by name.
—Psalm 147:4.

I take the Bible seriously. I feel it presents something vast that I am not vast enough to comprehend, but I know, nonetheless, the vastness is there. I often feel I'm in a car from which the universe is hidden. There is more going on than I know. But the Bible presents pinholes into which I can see beyond. The Bible is a whole series of pinholes through which the vastness of the heavens can be observed.

God has named the stars. He knows how many of them there are. These thoughts were present when I had opened the Gideon Bible that morning in Willcox, Arizona—The presence of the Lord was there in the pages of his book.

Now I wanted a job knowing the names of the stars. I would like to look into the directory. Are they in alphabetical order? Are they listed in order of their regions? Their placement within the continents of the universe?

Praise him you heavens, and you waters above the heavens. —Psalm 148:4.

I suspect there is a sea in outer space of heaven—in the heavens of heavens. I mentioned this once at a Bible study, and someone said there would not be a sea in heaven because it represented the nations, or the unruliness of sin. I was sorry to hear that, but the thought of a shore with boat rides still seemed a possibility. There can be the redemption of water. Sometimes I see the night sky like string lights on a seaside pavilion. That's what I see when I stand in the yard at my son's house in Texas. There are a few yard lights of other houses in the distance, but otherwise, it is dark in the rural place where they live. That's where I see the stars and think of the host of names that God had to think up when he named them. You'd think they'd just be excess, because of the great number of them. What would be the reason to name them? — They are more than the dust particles in all the dust devils that have stirred up the deserts of the world. They are the moths of heaven.

Christianity seems to me a relationship with a person — Jesus Christ, who died for my sins that I may approach God covered in the blood of Christ, and be acceptable to him — That is the Mark Line among the mark lines I feel as I cross the earth. The Matterhorn of the cross, if that is the summit of the earth. No, it's Mt. Everest. Actually, it's Mt. Chimborazo in Ecuador because the bulge of the earth at the equator pushes it above Everest.

The fact that Jesus had to die on the cross seems reasonable to me. Just look at the history of man. Cruelty. War. Misery. Dominance. Give a man power and he becomes a dictator. Give a man authority in his house and he wants several wives, ignoring their need for meaning and a quality of life. It is not history. It is us that make history. We are revealed in the acts of our history. It's what I hear in the voices on the road.

I can name a star, and say, you are there, though when I look again several nights later, it has migrated to another place, though it is the earth moving also, and the mark lines that travel with the earth. Or maybe it is the earth that travels with them. Maybe the stars have several names. In their moving, they are like those trucks — those great ships that pass on the highway in the night, pulling off sometimes into port to ride out a storm of gale-force winds off the Great Plains.

The Weight of Air

> The dullest instructional prose with the right light thrown on it, can acquire the gleam ... of insight. | Louis Menand, *Notable Quotables*

I bought bath soap on my last trip to Walmart — a three-bar package. As I unwrapped the first bar, I felt a concave bottom. I felt the other bars through the wrapping and found they all had concave bottoms. The manufacturer had found a way to make the package look the same and cost the same, but to give less soap to the customer. It probably was the same as buying two and a half bars — which bothered me —

It's not as if I, myself, were not guilty of giving less than I should from time to time. But I don't want to remember my own shortcomings. I prefer to remember the shortcomings of others. Wall Street, for instance, that has walked off with investors' money. Students, for instance, whom I suspected of taking their papers from the Internet. Cheating themselves, actually, leaving air pockets in their brains where synapses would have fired as they thought of what to say, comparing materials, synthesizing. They were not as interested in brain growth as in short-cutting. The way I moved into a house and found the short-cuts that had been taken. Plastic washers under the kitchen sink instead of brass, which I had to have replaced when they leaked. Or the floors they varnished without sanding the old varnish, so that the new layer began to flake as soon as I walked across it. And the new sander didn't remove the base boards, so I now have the scrape marks of his sander. The gutter man did not paint the fascia before he installed the new gutters, which were slimmer than the old gutters, and the old paint, a different color than the house, showed. When I called him, he refused to do anything.

What if Monet lad left a hole in his water lilies? Or Renoir left an opening in his seascape to thwart the rolling waves. What if, in the fifteenth century, Mateo Di Giovanni left a hole when he painted *The Massacre of the Innocents* — a hole through which they could have escaped? Or what if he left a hole where the red angels hovered over *St. Augustine's Vision of St. Jerome and John the Baptist* — red angels that looked like small red devils and gave thought to the thin line that separates oppositions.

Maybe the soap was not shoddy, or not quite up to snuff. Maybe it was a spiritual act—the way old Hopi and Navajo bowls had a hole in them so the spirit could get out.

Martin Luther found a hole in the church and posted his thesis on the Wittenberg door—The just shall live by faith—Galatians 3:10.

Enoch found a hole in his life when he "was no more"—Genesis 5:24. A story picked up in Hebrews 11:5—"By faith Enoch was translated that he should not see death, and was not found, because God had translated him; for before his translations he had this testimony, that he pleased God."

Einstein looked at hard science and found a hole that he called *relativity*. Physicists looked at space and came up with worm holes and black holes. Essayists looked at writing and came up with wanderings that the essay allows. Pliny. St. Augustine. Pascal. Montaigne. Pepys. The myriad of wandering thought-lines to follow their *relativities*.

From my office window in Gambier, I can see through the trees to a hill in the distance. There is a road coming down the hill. I see the headlights of a car because it is early, and the day is overcast, raining actually. The lights give evidence to a car I would not otherwise see on the gray road through the gray woods in the distance. On a sunny day, without headlights, I would not see the car coming down the hill, curving around a field until it comes to another road and stops before turning right or left or climbs the hill beside the window where I work.

The truth of the car on the road is changed by circumstance—a day that is dark enough for headlights. The car's presence is noticed because of the effect of something else (the weather) upon it—the way light rays are warped by gravity, which a black hole has in abundance—which gives evidence of the black hole—the way the physicists know the black hole is there by its effect on something else [light].

A car descends a hill through the trees with its headlights on. The lights are of a different nature than the woods and the ground over which the car passes. The headlights are intangible. Abstract. Not always there. They are separate from the physical world through which they pass. They are small yellow eyes. They are holes of light.

I know the road as truth. It is fact. It is there. I can see it from my window. I have traveled it. But it has not always been there. And may not necessarily always be. Maybe at one time it was an animal path. A wagon path. A shortcut. The truth of the road is not the truth of traveling a road.

Does truth possess an instrument only it can play? Or does it possess the only instrument it can play?

The glass in the windows where I stand is leaded with rectangles as if upright bars of soap that have not been diminished by the manufacturer's new policy of down sizing.

Soap is a program in installments.

Transverse Orientation

> Man and his authentic stay on earth exchange a reciprocity of proofs. |
> Stéphane Mallarmé, "The Reverie of a French Poet," from *Divagations*

Late one fall, on my way back to Kansas City from California on another trip, I passed through northern Arizona on I-40. There were times I slowed the car to see the land, the early yellow sun on the yellow rocks of a highway embankment, the yellow flowers on the chaparral, the yellow leaves on a few trees in a ravine where the highway crossed eye-level to them. It is that idea of memory. The uniqueness of it evident in writing. It is in the written word that these evidences are found. It is in the written word that that essay exists. Its multiplicities are foregoing. Transformed and preserved.

My place is in the passing terrain. I put on my moth wings. I fly ground-level. I am careful when I travel. I have a file box in the front seat I cover with a pillow and blanket as though someone is riding with me, asleep. The back windows are tinted and difficult to see in at night. I also cover the back windows with strips of cloth so anyone walking past the car cannot see in, even if they tried. I only stop at lighted, monitored rest stops with other cars for a few hours rest. I sleep with my cell phone. I sleep in my moth wings.

There are dimensions not realized until one takes possession. How often I dreamed there were other floors to the houses I lived in. Other stories. As there are stories on the road. Upper roads. Ascending stairs reached through driving to upper rooms or upper floors you don't know are there until you reach them. As sometimes when I am writing something, something else comes. My work dovetails into one another. Why this interstice? This interslice? This interstate? Why this language that has all this distance to come through?—all the turns—looking little like its first self when it arrives.

When I travel, sometimes I can see other trips, usually old USIS travels, when it was still in operation: Germany. Italy. Syria. Jordan. A travel-grant research trip to Caesarea and Turkey. A People to People jaunt to China. A sabbatical trip to Australia, New Zealand, and a museum on the northern edge of Antarctica, where there was a frightening and claustrophobic video of a seal swimming under an ice shelf.

What if I short-cut the long lines of my journey? Like the package of soap I bought at Walmart. I feel the road is more mathematical than I know, just as the old mounds. I've seen the grid lines of large cities from a plane at night. The old computer my grandson and I tore open that reminded me of those cities from a plane at night. What seems a gnarl in my hands is an ordinary aliquot in the Maker's—a number divisible into another without a remainder.

The diminishing of what I have known is upon me. Has always been with me. I just wasn't a part of the diminishment until now. I stop at another Walmart for a bottle of aspirin. A small travel bottle of aspirin in a cardboard box too big for it. Inside the bottle is a large wad of cotton. Beneath that, a carbon-and-silica-gel peg ["Absorbent for freshness"], in the open spaces of the bottle ["Do not eat."]. And finally, the small amount of aspirin. Thirty-two minute, yellow aspirin huddled in the bottom of the bottle — little animals huddling together in the back of a cave.

It seems our inconsistencies, travesties, and contradictions are part of our fabric.

Touch me not; for I am not yet ascended to my Father. — John 20:17.

Jesus met them saying, All hail. And they came and held him by the feet. — Matthew 28:9.

Behold my hands and my feet, that it is I myself; handle me, and see; for a spirit does not have flesh and bones. — Luke 24:39.

Then he said to Thomas, Reach here your finger and behold my hands; and reach here your hand, and thrust it into my side. — John 20:27.

Touch me. Don't touch. These *wobblinesses*. This angular relationship to the light. Because I drift into the isolation of travel to bring into place the connections to other places. I think of Marcel Duchamp's *Nude Descending a Staircase* in which the bones of the nude seem to become the descending stairs, and the boards of the stairs seem the bones of the body in a physical exchange of structure. The whole painting is a dissemination of two architectures. It is a flight of moths. I feel the constituency of words. Their noisy encumbrances on the road. The separation of paper doll from book. The breaking apart of seed planted in the soil of the field. The broken tools with which I have to plow.

www.ingramcontent.com/pod-product-compliance
Lightning Source LLC
Chambersburg PA
CBHW020654230426
43665CB00008B/437